Avoid Small-Business Hell

Avoid Small-Business Hell

Jack Borden

PRICE: $16.95 (3559/he   )

Self-Counsel Press
(a division of)
International Self-Counsel Press Ltd.
USA   Canada

Self-Counsel Press acknowledges the financial support of the Government of Canada through the Canada Book Fund for our publishing activities.

Printed in Canada.

First edition: 2015

Library and Archives Canada Cataloguing in Publication

Borden, Jack, author
    Avoid small business hell / Jack Borden.

(Business series)
Issued in print and electronic formats.

ISBN 978-1-77040-251-5 (paperback).—ISBN 978-1-77040-998-9 (epub).—ISBN 978-1-77040-999-6 (kindle)

    1. Small business. I. Title. II. Series: Self-Counsel business series
HD2341.B67 2015   658.02'2   C2015-903694-1
                                            C2015-903695-X

Self-Counsel Press
(a division of)
International Self-Counsel Press Ltd.

Bellingham, WA   North Vancouver, BC
USA   Canada

Contents

Samples

Worksheets

Notice to Readers

Every effort is made to keep this publication as current as possible. However, the author, the publisher, and the vendor of this book make no representations or warranties regarding the outcome or the use to which the information in this book is put and are not assuming any liability for any claims, losses, or damages arising out of the use of this book. The reader should not rely on the author or the publisher of this book for any professional advice. Please be sure that you have the most recent edition.

Acknowledgments

Dedicated to my wife, Elaine, who has been dragged through Small-Business Hell a few times, thanks to me. She has stuck by me through all of our ups and downs in business and is surely the backbone of the success of my numerous ventures.

Foreword

The publisher and I really struggled with the name for this book. When I first proposed the name *Avoid Small-Business Hell* it raised a few questions and a few eyebrows. Just what did I mean by these words? Is there really a place called "Small-Business Hell"? Yes, there really is such a place, and I am here to tell you that as a small-business entrepreneur, a trip into Small-Business Hell is something you want to avoid.

The words "Small-Business Hell" best describe the situation that many small businesses find themselves in from time to time. You just need to conjure up the image of what hell would really be like and then apply it to your situation if something seriously went wrong with your business.

I have been in Small-Business Hell more than once; therefore, everything I am writing in this book comes from my experiences or from the stories I have heard from other small-business entrepreneurs. The reason I am writing this book is to teach other small-business owners how to avoid Small-Business Hell. If I can save one person or one business from a devastating trip into Small-Business Hell, then the effort of writing this book will be well worthwhile.

Throughout the book you will see in bold and italics where I have inserted comments from readers, comments from small-business entrepreneurs, and real life small-business experiences. I hope you enjoy this diversion from theory to reality that takes place throughout the book.

Reader

So Jack, have you ever been in Small-Business Hell?

Jack's response

Yes I have, a few times, so I am writing this book based on personal experience. I am not going to say, "Unfortunately, I have been in Small-Business Hell" because sometimes a trip into Small-Business Hell is a beneficial experience as long as you can survive both business wise and personally, and return to prosperity sooner rather than later.

Introduction

This is a book about all the aspects of small business from starting one to operating one. What is a small business? Many of us think that a small business is owned and operated by an employer who has only a few employees that provide products and/or services in the local community. Governments around the world have various definitions of what a small business is in order to determine whether a business may be eligible for small-business programs. Many other agencies have their own definitions.

As far as this book is concerned, I prefer a very broad definition of a small business: An independently owned and operated business where the owner(s) exercise(s) close control over operations and decisions. The equity is not publicly traded and business financing is provided by the owner(s) and/or personally guaranteed by the owner(s). Typically, a small business employs fewer than 100 workers, but this is not a hard and fast rule. Most small businesses have annual sales revenue of less than $25 million. Although this book is for all small businesses it is really focused on the "smaller" small business: Businesses that employ one or more employees and have sales anywhere from a $100,000 to a few million dollars. Therefore, if your existing or proposed business fits into this very broad definition of small business, then this book is a must read for you.

Other important definitions used throughout the book are as follows:

- **Entrepreneur:** One who organizes and assumes the risk of a business or an enterprise.

- **Small-business entrepreneur:** One who organizes and assumes the risk of a small business.

- **Small-Business Hell:** A place where small-business entrepreneurs find themselves when something has gone terribly wrong and where the business and/or entrepreneur are facing significant challenges. Small-Business Hell is a period of time when a business is facing extremely difficult challenges and these challenges have put the owners into a position of extreme stress and worry. The business is in a state of jeopardy where even the survival of the business and the health and well-being of the owners may be put into question. I came up with this term a few years ago and it is based on my 40-plus years of small-business experience.

- **Small-Business Heaven:** A place where small-business entrepreneurs find themselves in when everything has gone right in their business for an extended period of time. All the customers' objectives are being met, sales are on target or ahead of budget, costs and expenses are on target or under budget, and profits are in the range of good to excellent. Just reading these words should bring feelings of joy and satisfaction to all small-business entrepreneurs.

Getting your business into Small-Business Heaven is no easy task, as most entrepreneurs will attest. There are a lot of things that need to go right in a business in order to arrive at the pearly gates of Small-Business Heaven. There is no magic formula; there are no get-rich-quick schemes; there is only hard work, dedication, and smart business practices — that's what it takes to be successful.

No matter what a small-business entrepreneur does, and no matter how well the business is managed, almost every small business ends up in Small-Business Hell at least once. This book is about achieving all the things you need to do in order to be successful and to reach the pinnacle of Small-Business Heaven, as well as how to avoid the trip into Small-Business Hell. If, for whatever reason, you do find yourself in

Small-Business Hell, this book should help you navigate your way out of purgatory and back into Small-Business Heaven.

Reader

Whoa! Wait a minute. Are you telling me that if my business gets into difficulty and into Small-Business Hell that it could put my health and well-being in jeopardy?

Jack's response

That is exactly what I am telling you.

Reader

OK. Now you really have my attention.

After reading these words I hope you are saying to yourself: "I never, never, never want to get into Small-Business Hell. I will do whatever it takes to avoid the trip into Small-Business Hell. I pity those small-business owners who have gone there."

How do businesses get into Small-Business Hell in the first place? I can tell you, no entrepreneur plans on getting into trouble but almost every small-business owner ends up in Small-Business Hell at least once in his or her career.

Reader

Why do businesses end up in Small-Business Hell? What did the owners do wrong that they ended up there? Okay, I am going to read this book because I will do everything I can do to avoid going to Small-Business Hell and taking my business with me.

Jack's response

Good! Please keep reading.

There are likely thousands of reasons why a business ends up in Small-Business Hell and they are all devastating. Of all these reasons they can typically be classified into one of these four categories:

- Financial
- Sales
- Operations
- Personal

More specifically, let's look at a few real examples of business challenges that could force a business and its owners into Small-Business Hell:

- Business is losing money.

- Lack of sales to sustain the business.

- Too much competition such as a new competitor took away a chunk of the business sales that were needed to keep the business going.

- Entered into a contract or an obligation that is creating a significant loss for the business.

- Misjudged the economy and now the business is devastated by an immediate downturn in the industry.

- Key employee has quit and then advised that he or she is going into competition with the business.

- Customer who owes your business a substantial amount of money has gone bankrupt.

- Flaw in the production process has forced the immediate shutdown of the production line.

- You have, your spouse has, and/or a close family member has encountered a major personal setback and this is affecting your ability to operate your business.

These are just a few examples of things that could happen in your life or the life of your business that may thrust you immediately into Small-Business Hell, typically without warning.

Throughout this book, you will find real small- and big-business stories. These stories will be told in the first person but the first person is not me, they are entrepreneurs I have met and who have told their stories to me, or their stories have been relayed to me by others. Let's look at an example:

Small-business story

I lost my best and biggest customer to my competitors and I just found out today. Over the past few months I have invested heavily into my business in anticipation of new orders from this customer and now the opportunity is gone. Gone! Now I have to lay off employees. I borrowed money and I don't know how I am going to pay back the bank. I am in trouble. Everything was great yesterday but today I am in Small-Business Hell. What did I do wrong?

Jack's response

This looks like a case of putting the cart ahead of the horse. What were you thinking hiring additional employees and making capital and inventory investments without a valid and secure contract from your customer? Yep, you are in Small-Business Hell. Read on to find out how to get out of Small-Business Hell or, more importantly, how you could have avoided the trip in the first place.

I aim to make this book extremely interesting to all small-business entrepreneurs and to keep your attention throughout the entire book. Business books are usually long and boring and you have to work hard to extract the information that is important to you and your business. This book as well as my previous book, *Faster, Cheaper, Better: Starting and Operating a Business in the Trades*, were written specifically for small-business entrepreneurs and are intended to provide you with the information you need to be very successful. Please note that some of the information in this book overlaps with the information provided in *Faster, Cheaper, Better*.

1
Small-Business Hell

After I published *Faster, Cheaper, Better*, I often heard from experienced businesspersons who commented, "Where were you 25 years ago when I was starting my business? That's when I really needed you!" However, younger entrepreneurs seem to be less interested even though they are the ones who could derive the most benefit from reading my book. It doesn't make sense, does it? Do all young entrepreneurs go into business thinking that everything they touch will turn to gold and they can do no wrong? I think many do.

Experienced small-business entrepreneurs who may have taken a trip or two into Small-Business Hell are much more receptive to some advice from someone with a lot of small-business experience. No matter who you are, whether you are an experienced entrepreneur, or a person just starting out, or contemplating a venture as an entrepreneur, please take the time to learn some very valuable lessons. Hopefully investing a few hours into reading this book will save you and your business from the devastation of a trip into Small-Business Hell. Please take it from me, I wish I had had the benefit of this book when I started my life as a small-business entrepreneur back in the early 1970s.

I don't want to just focus on the negative; I want to focus on the positive aspects of the lessons to be learned in this book. After all, this is what life is all about: Learning from experience. The question is, do you want to learn from just your own experiences, or would you like to learn from the experiences of others with the hope of not having to repeat their mistakes?

Reader

The competition in my industry is fierce. Some of my competitors must be working for peanuts based on the prices they are offering to their customers. I don't know how we are all going to survive.

Jack's response

In life, as a small-business entrepreneur, you are guaranteed three things: death, taxes, and competition. Love your competitors or hate them, it is competition that is the backbone of the free-enterprise system. It is competition that will drive you to be the best that you can be. If you fail to compete, your business will fail; it is that simple.

Another very important aspect of this book is how to avoid the trip into Small-Business Hell in the first place, but if you do find yourself there, I will discuss how to get out of it. Typically there are only two ways out of Small-Business Hell: You can manage your way out, or you can declare bankruptcy or take some other similar form of action to shut down your business. For many, the easiest way out is to abandon the business; the repercussions of this action can have a lifelong, devastating, negative impact. However, managing your way out of Small-Business Hell can be very rewarding and when you successfully exit it, you can chalk it up as the best small-business experience you can get and you will be better for it for the rest of your career.

Reader

Are you overexaggerating the impact a trip into Small-Business Hell will have on me and my business? You make it sound like it is the end of the world!

Jack's response

I have been in Small-Business Hell a few times and, trust me, if you can avoid the trip, you should. The most devastating part of a trip into Small-Business Hell is the impact it has on you, your personal life, and your family. Your business is supposed to provide you with a living and to allow you to have the lifestyle you envision. Personal tragedy has struck many families when a business is in Small-Business Hell. Maybe you even know someone who has experienced Small-Business Hell and the negative impact it had on him or her: Divorce, alcoholism, mental illness, sleep disorders, suicide, bankruptcy, negative impacts on one's personality, constant worry, and stress in relationships — just to name a few things that could happen. So no, I don't think I am overexaggerating the impact of a trip into Small-Business Hell. It really is HELL!

Reader

Okay, I am convinced. I want to avoid the trip into Small-Business Hell.

Jack's response

I like the way you think. Read on.

What makes a small business successful? Obviously if you have a successful small business the chances of being thrust into Small-Business Hell are much lower than if you are running a business that is on the edge of trouble or facing unidentified risks. There are only three aspects to every business; whether large or small:

1. You have to sell your product and/or services to meet the sales targets you have established for your business.

2. You have to produce your product and/or services for less than you sell them for with adequate margins to sustain your business and earn a fair and reasonable profit.

3. You have to account for your business, which means all aspects of the paperwork, such as finance, banking, management, invoicing, receivables, bookkeeping, accounting, and human resources.

That's it. That is all there is to having a successful business. Small-Business Heaven will occur if the following happens:

- Sales targets are met.

- Great production with room for good margins and profits.

- Well-managed business practices.

This all sounds too easy so why do so many businesses fail? Back to the three business basics:

- Lack of sales.
- Poor production, quality problems, high costs.
- Poor business-management practices.

Reader

So Jack, are you telling me if I want to have a successful business I need to have good sales, great production, and excellent business management?

Jack's response

Yes, this is what you need to do to be successful.

Reader

What if I do two out of three really well and fail at the other?

Jack's response

That's really easy to answer. Welcome to Small-Business Hell!

Now that you have a feel for what it may be like to be a small-business entrepreneur you have to ask yourself if you are really cut out for this type of career. There are many other choices. You can work for someone else in your chosen field and never have to worry about the risks related to owning your own business. After all, you can't be thrust into Small-Business Hell if you aren't a small-business entrepreneur. So there is the first word of advice on how to avoid the trip into Small-Business Hell: Do not become a small-business entrepreneur. There, that solved that problem!

I have defined the three basic components of every business:

- Sales
- Production/operations
- Accounting/paperwork

For the most part, every business that makes the trip into Small-Business Hell has had an issue that would fall into one of these three business components or some combination thereof. Of course, businesses are more complex than just the three primary business components. Every small business will usually deal with one or more of the following business matters as well:

- Customers

- Employees

- Suppliers and subcontractors

- Buying Faster, Cheaper, Better (more on this later)

- Partners

- Family

- Competition

- Risk

- Business planning

- Succession planning

All of these are extremely important and I will deal with every one of these subjects throughout the book.

Small-business story

I got involved in a business with two other partners. The business was in the recreation field and required a substantial investment to acquire the business. The business was quite diverse and involved an operations side as well as a development component. There came a time when the business had to make a substantial investment into infrastructure in the millions of dollars.

In the final analysis of the investment, we had to choose between two suppliers for the equipment. One supplier was $1 million less than its competitor (about 10 percent). We really wanted to go with the more expensive supplier but we opted for the lowest bid without really taking into consideration the downstream effect of this business decision. One year later the equipment failed, the supplier went broke, and it cost more than $2 million to make the necessary repairs. This was $2 million that we didn't have in the business, so as partners we all had to contribute more money.

It's hard to believe but this story actually gets worse. A few years later one of our competitors, who had the same (inferior) equipment, decided to rip it all out and replace its equipment with the brand that we should have bought in the first place. Therefore our competitor had all of this surplus equipment that was of no value to it so we decided that we should buy it for spare parts; after all, we could have the equipment for virtually nothing. Unfortunately, "virtually nothing" became another $500,000 by the time we removed the equipment, packaged it, transported it, and stored it at our site.

Now you may not believe this, but this story actually gets even worse. The following year we were approached by a competitor and it wanted to buy us out. We had to look very seriously at its offer as we had serious financial matters to deal with due to all of the additional costs related to the equipment that we had purchased. We had the business appraised and the buyer was prepared to pay the appraised price — less $10 million to replace the equipment that we had. The buyer's business policy was that it would only use the equipment that we should have purchased in the first place. We finally succumbed and accepted the buyer's offer. Hindsight, as we know, has 20/20 vision. At the time of our fateful decision, if we had taken the time to fully assess the situation, we would have determined that the higher priced supplier was actually a better solution in all ways — Faster, Cheaper, Better. But we didn't.

The final cost to the partners was losses in the millions and we sold the business for a loss. Our partnership was dissolved (and not amicably, I must say) and I am still paying off the debt that was left behind. All of this because of one business decision that was made that we didn't take the time to fully research and understand the downstream effect that this decision would have. We knew better and we certainly know better now. What happened to the surplus equipment that we had stored on our site? It went to the salvager's for scrap.

Jack's response

This is a real trip into Small-Business Hell that lasted for a few years for these entrepreneurs. I feel sorry for the partners in this business, but they made a mistake that cost them dearly. The partners did not recognize the magnitude of the decision they were making. They did not adequately research the equipment, and they did not analyze the potential downstream effects of their decision if something did go wrong.

What should they have done? They should have created a business plan for this major expansion to their business. The business plan needed to include a complete risk analysis, a project objective analysis, "what if" scenarios, a financial analysis, and options that *could have been considered to reduce the overall cost of the project that may have allowed them to buy the superior equipment in the first place. I am confident if they had gone this extra mile they would have found a way to purchase the equipment that they really wanted and they wouldn't have compromised and selected inferior equipment.*

Buyers who thoroughly analyze major purchases using the Faster, Cheaper, Better purchasing method will inevitably make better buying decisions than those who do not take the time to complete this process. I have dedicated a chapter in this book on how to buy Faster, Cheaper, Better so read on.

2

So You Want to Be
a Small-Business
Entrepreneur?

Being a small-business entrepreneur isn't for everyone but you will find
a number of small businesses throughout your community. As you will
see in the following list, small businesses are in numerous industries:

- Advertising

- Agriculture and farming

- Automotive

- Barbers and hairdressing

- Bed and breakfasts

- Bookkeepers, accountants, and financial advisors

- Consultants

- Contractors

- Drycleaners

- Education (special services and supply)
- Electronic industry including supply and repairs
- Health products and services
- Home maintenance services
- Home-related retail
- Industry and related supply sector
- Insurance
- Marine
- Music and entertainment
- Office supplies
- Pet supply and services
- Professional services
- Real estate
- Recreation
- Recycling
- Restaurants and other food-service businesses
- Retirement industry
- Suppliers
- Tourism
- Transport

The list is almost endless. The bottom line is that the economy would not function without small businesses as they are its backbone. You may deal with dozens if not hundreds of small businesses every year.

This chapter is not intended to scare or discourage you from pursuing your desire to become a small-business entrepreneur. The purpose is to give you better insight into what you are getting into and to ensure that you go into business with your eyes wide open. Where would the world be if it wasn't for people like you who are willing to take the risk to become small-business entrepreneurs?

Consider the topics in the following sections as you work through the two worksheets included at the end of this chapter. The worksheets can be printed by accessing them through the download kit link included at the end of this book.

1. Risks

What is the risk of becoming a small-business entrepreneur? In life we take risks every day — when we cross the street, when we drive somewhere, or when we participate in activities. But what are business risks? At the top of the list is financial. When you say you are a risk taker in business it means you are prepared to risk your hard-earned money on a business venture. If the venture fails, you are going to lose money. Are you prepared to take this risk?

Other business risks relate to sales. What if you don't make enough in sales to sustain your business? If you don't, you are going to go broke. Are you prepared to take this risk? Give this some very serious thought before you answer question 1 in Worksheet 1 at the end of this chapter.

2. Are You a Self-Starter and a Hard Worker?

Give some thought to the people you know. You probably know some hard workers and some slackers. You may know some people who motivate themselves and those who need a kick in the butt to get moving in the morning. There are also those people who have extremely good work ethics while others are more focused on other aspects of their lives.

Now you need to assess yourself. You need to be very honest with your self-appraisal. Successful small-business entrepreneurs drive themselves; no one needs to prod them. Successful small-business owners have an exemplary work ethic and are not afraid to work hard. I don't mean they just work hard physically; they work with a focus on every task they undertake and are driven to succeed. Do you?

Small-business story

My small business was committed to a contract on a major project up north. In the beginning this project looked like it was going to be a winner but after a few months everything you can imagine went wrong. We had major problems with the customer, local unions, suppliers, employees — almost everything had gone wrong. I was going to lose hundreds of thousands of dollars.

Not one to give up, I solved the problems with the union and that solved the problems with the employees. I met with the suppliers and got that straightened away but what was I going to do about the most difficult customer I have ever dealt with? I was sitting in my office contemplating the situation when my phone rang. It was my customer. He said he was phoning me to advise me that they had just been bought out. The new company owner recognized the problems on the project and he wanted me to be part of the team to get the project back on track. He asked if I could meet him on site the next day.

How did things turn out? The project went on for another year. We became a major part of the solution and instead of losing money, we did very well on the project in the end. Some things turn out okay as long as you are prepared to hang in there and work hard — good old stick-to-itiveness works every time.

3. Leadership

You've probably heard the saying, "lead, follow, or get the hell out of the way." One out of five people is a potential leader; three out of five people will make good workers; and one out of five people you don't want to have working for you. So who are you? Are you the one out of five who naturally leads people? Are you a take charge kind of person? Do people look up to you and respect you? Do you have good interpersonal skills with your colleagues, family, and friends?

Small-business story

One of my early introductions to the passion of small-business entrepreneurs was when my boss told me that once you catch the small-business entrepreneur fever you will never want to work for someone else again. He caught on to being a small-business entrepreneur when his mother sent him out to sell flowers door to door when he was a child and he got to keep a percentage of the sales he made. That was it — he was hooked.

4. Your Specific Field of Expertise

Consider whether or not you are an expert in your specific field. Are you good at what you do? Do you pay attention to details? Do you think you can operate your business better than your competition?

Small-business story

I bought a new business in an industry with which I was not familiar. I know now that my business plan was primarily based on inexperience and wishful thinking. If I knew then what I know now I would have paid substantially less for the business than I did, and it would have made the first few years in business much more rewarding.

Jack's response

Focus on your business plan and the reality of business, not wishful thinking. Management by wishful thinking is a surefire way to end up in Small-Business Hell.

5. Sell, Sell, Sell

You will need to be able to sell your service or product. Consider whether you are a natural when it comes to sales. Are you confident in your ability to close deals? Are you comfortable in competitive selling situations? Are you comfortable dealing with customers? You will need to be a good negotiator as well as have a passion about the products and services you are selling.

6. Accounting and Financials

Most small-business entrepreneurs don't have formal training in the fields of accounting, finance, and bookkeeping. How do you handle your personal finances? Can you prepare and stick to budgets? Are you organized when it comes to filing information and tracking expenses? You may not be an expert in this field and you may plan on hiring someone to undertake accounting and bookkeeping — maybe your spouse or a partner — but are you prepared to learn the fundamentals of business accounting practices and job-costing procedures? This is critical if you really want to understand what is happening in your business.

7. Responsible and Reliable

Are you responsible and reliable? These personality traits are fundamental to your success in business. Your customers, employees, suppliers, colleagues, and business associates will expect a lot from you and they want to deal with someone who is reliable and responsible, someone they can depend on. Are there any personal things going on in your life that make you irresponsible and unreliable?

8. Life Changing Commitment

Don't take the move from employee to small-business entrepreneur lightly. Work hours of 9:00 a.m. to 5:00 p.m. will be a thing of the past. Leaving your work behind when you leave the store, office, or shop will be impossible. You can't let your business control you but it will play a major role in your everyday life.

Is your family prepared for you to undertake this life changing commitment? Families of small-business entrepreneurs inevitably get involved in the family business; even if it is just in a supporting role, they will still be impacted by this life changing commitment. Consider carefully the questions in Worksheet 2.

Small-business story

Job prospects in our community didn't look good so I decided to go out on my own and set up my own business. I didn't want to be an employee anymore; I wanted to be my own boss. That was ten years ago. Although I have gone through some difficult times in my business I have worked hard, I have excellent employees, I have great customers, and my business is now a success. Personally, the business has been tough on the family from time to time but we are far better off financially than we would be if I had stayed working as an employee for somebody else. I am now a tried and true small-business entrepreneur and I wouldn't change my business life for anything.

Jack's response

Another success story in the world of small business. This could be you!

9. Money

Why do you want to become a small-business entrepreneur? To make more money should be the answer. If you are not prepared to set the bar extremely high for yourself, and to strive to earn significantly more money than you would as an employee, then you may not be cut out for self-employment. This isn't about greed; this is about you and your business being very profitable and the profits from your labors providing you with an enhanced lifestyle. That's how it works for successful small-business entrepreneurs.

10. Challenges and Heartaches

Unfortunately, challenges and heartaches come with the territory when you are a small-business entrepreneur. Things that may happen in your business will have a greater impact on you than on your employees. Remember, employees can walk away, albeit they may walk away without a job. You can't walk away; at least not without doing significant damage to your reputation and financial security.

Before you begin a career as a small-business entrepreneur you should answer and grade the questions in Worksheet 1 to get an idea of where you stand. This is not a scientifically proven test but it can act as a good indicator of whether or not you are suited to be a small-business entrepreneur. (You can print a copy of this worksheet by using the link to the download kit provided at the end of this book.)

Keep in mind that a low score in this analysis identifies an individual as an excellent employee as well; an excellent employee who has the alternative to become a small-business entrepreneur.

Reader

Jack, I took the test, and I believe I answered every question honestly. Sorry, but I am putting your book away for another time. The time is just not right for me or my family to take these risks.

Jack's response

I am sorry to hear that, but I am glad that you recognize up front what is best for you and your family. There is an employer out there who is looking for a logical person just like you. You will make an excellent employee for some business and there may be an opportunity for you to pursue a career as a small-business entrepreneur sometime in the future.

If you answer "no" to any of the questions in Worksheet 2, then regardless of your score you should abandon any thoughts of becoming a small-business entrepreneur. Again, this is not intended to scare away potential small-business entrepreneurs, but to ensure that you are making the right decision for you and your family.

Reader

Jack, I took the test and my score was very low. It looks like I may only be suited to become a small-business entrepreneur. I struggled a bit

Worksheet 1
Are You Suited to Be a Small-Business Entrepreneur?

Circle the number that fits your personality:

1: I agree; this defines me and my situation.
3: Neutral.
5: This is definitely not me.

1.	I am a risk taker.		1	2	3	4	5
2.	I am self-motivated and a hard worker; I don't need anyone to lead me.		1	2	3	4	5
3.	I am a leader and motivator to others.		1	2	3	4	5
4.	I am extremely adept at my specific field of expertise.		1	2	3	4	5
5.	I can sell myself, my expertise, my products, and/or my services.		1	2	3	4	5
6.	I am an excellent accountant, financial and cost analyst, and office organizer.		1	2	3	4	5
7.	I am extremely responsible and reliable in all aspects of my life.		1	2	3	4	5
8.	I am prepared to undertake a life-changing commitment to become a small-business entrepreneur.		1	2	3	4	5
9.	I am motivated by money and I want to make a lot of it.		1	2	3	4	5
10.	I am prepared for the challenges and heartaches that small-business entrepreneurs inevitably encounter.		1	2	3	4	5

Score Analysis

10 to 20: You could make an excellent small-business entrepreneur.

21 to 30: You may want to reconsider becoming a small-business entrepreneur.

31 to 50: Spruce up your résumé and apply for jobs to become an employee.

with Worksheet 2 but in the end my partner and I answered the questions together and I will have the support I need to pursue my goal of becoming a small-business entrepreneur. I am ready to read on.

Jack's response

Welcome to the land of small-business entrepreneurs. Successful business owners are a rare breed and I wish you luck in your new business, whatever it may be. May good sales be upon you; may you meet all of your customers' objectives; and may you profit and prosper in your new enterprise.

For successful business owners, there will be some very good times but along with the good times there will inevitably be some challenging times. It is these challenging times that make businesspeople stronger and better at what they do as long as they are prepared to make the commitment to succeed no matter what the challenges may be and to learn from their mistakes.

If you can pass the tests, and you still think that being a small-business entrepreneur may be right for you, keep reading.

Worksheet 2
Are You Ready to Make Personal Sacrifices?

Answer yes or no to the following questions:

1. Does my spouse or partner, and/or family support my decision to become a small-business entrepreneur?

2. Do I want to sacrifice a significant part of my life, my free time, and my personal freedom for the sake of my business?

3. Am I prepared to undertake a life of worry and fret about my business knowing that there will be bad times along with the good times?

4. Will I be able to handle the stress that comes with money issues and will I be able to cope with the monetary risks?

5. Am I prepared to put my personal life and stability at risk?

3

Prepare a Business Plan

Your business plan is going to be the road map for your business. A detailed plan along with financial projections is going to give you an insight into whether this is going to be a viable operation or not. Your business plan is going to set realistic goals, objectives, and projections and will define how you are going to meet them.

Whether you are preparing a business plan for a new business or an existing business the same basic rules apply. For a new business, your projections are based on your best estimates. For existing businesses, projections should be based on historical operating information. For existing businesses planning to expand and/or move into new market areas, your projections are going to be based on your best estimates. No matter whether your business is new or established you should always have a properly prepared five-year business plan and it should be updated at least once per year. If you consistently meet your projections, that's good for you. If you consistently miss your projections, it's time to review your plan; otherwise, you could find yourself in Small-Business Hell before you know it.

Your business plan, at this stage, may be fictional but keep in mind when you put it into action you will be held to account for every last word and commitment you have made. You must be realistic and honest with yourself. No one has ever implemented a business plan that showed that the business had no chance of succeeding; if they did, they must have had money and time to burn! However, many business plans are created using wishful thinking and they project some great results but they are not based in reality. Proceeding into business with a flawed business plan would be your first step towards failure and possible financial ruin and certainly a trip into Small-Business Hell. This book is all about how to succeed not how to fail and the very first step is a business plan that is realistic, implementable, and clearly demonstrates how your business is going to succeed and be successful.

Small-business story

Before I started my own business I was a manager in a very large business with a very good salary. I wanted to be a small-business entrepreneur so I left my job to start my own business. I knew there would be a start-up curve but unfortunately I did not do a good job on my business plan. I needed to change my lifestyle, my wife needed to adjust her spending habits, and my children had to lower their expectations until such time as my new business was successful and could afford to pay me what I was used to earning. Unfortunately none of us made these adjustments, my personal salary needs exceeded what the company could provide, and within three years I was bankrupt.

My mistake was not creating a business plan that was workable and not recognizing that I had to change my salary expectations when first starting out. If I had done this, the business would have succeeded and likely within five years I would have been earning more than I did in my salaried job.

1. Financial Projections

I prefer to start my business plans with *pro forma* financial projections that are made up of two financial documents — a balance sheet and a statement of earnings (income statement). The easiest way to create the *pro forma* financial projections is to build an Excel spreadsheet. (The download kit that comes with this book includes some basic financial statements that will assist you with the preparation of this part of your business plan.)

For those of you who are adept at or have a good working knowledge of basic bookkeeping and accounting you can skip this section of the book. For those of you who are new to bookkeeping and accounting, the following is a fundamental guideline. Remember if you proceed with your business plan, you must acquire a good working knowledge of accounting and bookkeeping. Being able to read the financial status of your business is critical if you expect to be successful.

1.1 Balance sheet

The balance sheet is a snapshot of the financial state of your business at a specific date in time. It lists your assets, liabilities, and shareholders' equity. A balance sheet is exactly what the name implies: Assets = Liabilities + Shareholders' Equity; they are balanced.

Examples of assets are cash in the bank, accounts receivable, inventory, equipment, land, and buildings. Assets are broken down into *current assets*, which are assets that can readily be converted into cash; and *noncurrent assets* that are fixed or longer term.

Examples of liabilities are lines of credit, accounts payable, and bank loans. Liabilities are broken down into *current liabilities*, which are liabilities that are due to be paid within one year or less; and *noncurrent liabilities* that are repaid over a longer term. Shareholders' loans to the company to provide it with working capital can be listed under noncurrent liabilities.

Shareholders' equity is the value of your investment in your business. It is made up of capital stock for companies and retained earnings.

1.2 Statement of earnings and retained earnings

The statement of earnings is a record of the financial transactions that have taken place in your business over a defined period of time. The statement of earnings lists your sales, cost of sales, expenses, and the resultant income. Retained earnings are also tracked from year to year.

- **Revenue or sales:** Revenue derived from selling goods and services.

- **Cost of sales:** Costs related directly to sales which typically wouldn't be incurred if there weren't any sales (e.g., project materials and labor).

- **Gross profit:** The profit before taking expenses into account.

- **Expenses:** Overhead costs which are incurred even if there weren't any sales (e.g., rent, management salaries, accounting, and bookkeeping).

- **Earnings before income taxes:** Earnings are recorded prior to determining income taxes owing. You will have earnings if your revenue exceeds your cost of sales and your expenses. You will have earnings if you have produced what you sold for less than you sold it for.

- **Income taxes:** If you are making money, you must make an allowance for income taxes.

- **Retained earnings:** Basically earnings that are retained in your business that are not paid out to the owners.

Before you start inputting your information into the worksheets included on the download kit, try this exercise: Assume you have been in business for one year and this is the status of your business. Based on the information in Sample 1, create a balance sheet and a statement of earnings.

Remember, this is fiction not reality. I am providing some large round numbers. Try breaking them down into the various secondary categories on the worksheet. For example, break the sales down into contract sales, material sales, and labor sales. If you are having trouble understanding this now would be the time to seek some accounting or bookkeeping advice and training. If you are going to become a small-business entrepreneur, you are going to need these skills.

Sample 1
Statement of Earnings

Sales	$1,000,000
Cost of sales	$800,000
Gross profit	$200,000
Expenses	$100,000
Earnings	$100,000

Now it's time to create some financial projections for your business. You may find this to be a grueling exercise but it is far better to deal with it now in a semi-realistic sense than to find out a few months or a year or two after you start your business that your projections were fiction at best. See Sample 2.

Sample 2
Balance Sheet

Current assets	$310,000
Noncurrent assets	$50,000
Current liabilities	$100,000
Noncurrent liabilities	$50,000
Shareholders' loan	$100,000
Shareholders' equity	$10,000
Net earnings	$100,000

- **Revenue or sales:** How much do you expect to sell in your first year in business? You will need to provide details on the source of sales and how you are going to meet your sales targets in the actual business plan.

- **Cost of sales:** Obviously your cost of sales must be less than your sales. The percentage difference is going to be your margin on sales. What is standard for your industry? Is it 10 percent (not enough), 15 percent (a tight margin in most businesses), or more than 20 percent? You will need to back up your projections in your business plan.

- **Gross profit:** Equal to your percentage margin times your sales. For example, if you have sales of $1 million at a 20 percent margin, your gross profit will be $200,000.

- **Expenses:** Don't underestimate your expenses. Most importantly, determine how much your business is going to pay you and include this in expenses. For smaller businesses you may anticipate working out in the field (working in a production role) and in this case a portion of your wages may be included in cost of sales. What is a reasonable percentage for expenses in your industry? It is typically around 10 percent but this may vary from business to business and industry to industry.

- **Earnings before income taxes:** If your gross profit is 20 percent and your expenses are 10 percent, then your earnings before income taxes will be 10 percent. Think about this for a minute. For every dollar you make in sales you get to earn one thin dime. It doesn't sound like much does it? Think about how hard you are going to have to work for that one dime.

- **Income taxes:** After all that hard work you have to pay taxes on all those dimes you have busted your butt to earn. An allowance for taxes will depend on your federal, state or provincial, and local tax laws. You will need to consult a professional to determine the allowance you should make for current and future taxes.

- **Retained earnings:** In this scenario, assuming you are going to retain the earnings in your business, you now have $100,000 in retained earnings less whatever tax allowances you are going to make which could be anywhere from 0 to 25 percent or more. Now create your balance sheet and try to figure out where that $100,000 is because it's probably not in the bank.

- **Assets:** Your projections are for year one in your business so you are going to have some assets. You are going to have some money in the bank, you are going to have accounts receivable, and you may have bought some fixed assets.

- **Liabilities:** You may owe suppliers and employees for costs related to your sales. Have you set up a line of credit at the bank? List shareholders' loans here as well.

- **Shareholders' equity:** For the purposes of this exercise if you have earned $100,000 less tax allowances you will have this amount in retained earnings.

The beauty of the Excel spreadsheets is that you can do a number of "what ifs." Reduce your sales to $500,000 and double your salary and see what happens. Assume that you are not going to work in production and your entire salary is going to be overhead and see what happens. Keep doing "what ifs" until your projections become realistic.

2. Write Your Business Plan

The reason I like to do the *pro forma* projections before actually writing the plan is that the pro forma exercise immerses you into the business that you envision. Assuming you have done enough "what ifs," you should now have created a projected set of financial statements that you honestly believe are achievable. Now prove it to the best of your ability.

Remember, first you have to convince yourself, then you have to convince others who may be lending you money or investing in your business. You want readers of your plan, including yourself, to experience an ever-increasing level of confidence in you and your business as the business plan is read and understood. As a reader of a plan, I want to come away with the feeling that this is a plan that will work, it is the foundation for a successful business, and with a very high level of confidence in the principals and principles of the business.

Your business plan will likely be about five pages long plus your financial projections. For more complex businesses the plan may be longer and for simpler businesses it may be shorter.

The first step in writing your plan is to explain to the reader what your business is. This is critical. Keep in mind that others who may read your plan may not be familiar with your industry. You want your explanation to be clear and concise and about a page long. For example, after I read the first page of your business plan, I should be able to say, "I get it." I understand that this plan is a plan for a real business and I have a basic understanding of what the business is all about and what it does.

The second step is to tell the reader about yourself, who you are, and what your experience is in the industry. Explain why you are suited to be a small-business entrepreneur and why you want to be one.

You should focus on your uniqueness. It is unlikely that you are going to state in your business plan that there are another hundred competitors in your area just like you and you are going to be just like them. No! You are unique. Your business will be unique when compared to your competitors. Your approach to your customers will be unique when compared to your competitors. Your customers are going to want to deal with you because of your unique approach to your business. In fact, what makes you unique is that your focus is on meeting your customers' buying objectives. I can guarantee that most businesses cannot honestly make this statement.

Next, outline your goals and objectives, which include your mission statement, business principles, and values.

You will also need to describe how the business is going to operate. This means describing where the business is going to be located; the key people in the business; and what plans are there for employees, who they are, and what they will do.

This all sounds really good but the reader is going to want to know three more things:

- How are you going to sell your product or service?
- How are you going to produce it for less than you sell it for?

- How are you going to account for it?

A business cannot survive without enough sales to sustain it. A business suffering from a lack of sales will die a slow, agonizing death. The reader wants to know how you are going to get enough sales to not only sustain your business but enough sales to allow your business to be profitable, to grow, and to be successful. You will need to answer the following questions:

- What market research have you done?

- Who are your potential customers?

- How much do these potential customers buy?

- What is your relationship with these customers?

- Why are these customers going to buy from you and not your competition?

- How are you going to sell to these customers?

- How are you going to attract new customers?

- What geographic area are you going to cover?

- Are you going to specialize in any particular segment of your industry or are you going to provide a broader range of services?

Your sales summary and analysis should support the sales projections you have outlined in your business plan.

You have shown how you are going to make sales in your business; now you have to demonstrate how you are going to produce what you sold for less than you sold it for, at margins consistent with what you have shown in your financial projections. Ideally you have now convinced the reader that you can sell, you can produce what you sold for less than you sold it for, and you are going to demonstrate how you are going to account for it.

Referring to your financial *pro forma* projections you need to outline the business's requirement for working capital and how this working capital is going to be provided. If you reduce the amount of a bank line of credit, the amount of working capital should be increased by the same amount. For purposes of a plan with anticipated annual sales of $1 million, you could plan on providing between $100,000 and $200,000 in shareholders' loans to the company to use as working capital and to arrange a bank line of credit in the same amount. Do not, under any circumstances, create a plan for your business that does not provide adequate working capital. You will be doomed to Small-Business Hell before you start, and readers of the plan who you may want to invest in your business and/or lend you money will be the first to point this out.

Your initial plan should be for five years. It can be a real challenge to create a long-range plan at this stage of your business development. Make sure your first-year projections are as close to reality as possible and then project realistic and achievable growth for subsequent years.

If you proceed with going into business, it is very important to revisit your plan on a regular basis (at least once every six months) and to update your plan based on actual results versus projections. All of your projections will not be spot on, so updating it will bring it more closely in line with reality as the business moves forward.

There is an infinite amount of information on the Internet about business plans. Some of the information is useful and some is not. I suggest that you consult the Internet to do some basic research and then integrate what you have learned into your plan.

3. Financing

How are you going to finance your business? On day one you don't have any retained earnings so you have to rely on two things — working capital that you can put into the business, and bank financing. How much capital do you need? This needs to be clearly defined in your business plan. If you are extremely adept at the finance and administration side of the business, your financial projections will determine the working capital required for your business. If you are not adept in this area, you should seek some professional advice to assist you.

More importantly, where is your working capital contribution going to come from? Ideally you will have saved enough money in order to start your business so you don't have to rely on other sources. This usually isn't reality for most start-up businesses. Consider the following sources of working capital carefully and determine how best to put your plan together.

Your business must be adequately capitalized. If it is undercapitalized, even though you are making money, you could be forced out of business because you won't have enough money to pay your employees, suppliers, and other commitments. Consider the typical sources of capital and resultant implications in Sample 3.

Sample 3
Sources of Capital and the Implications of Each Source

$100,000	What to Consider
Self-funded without taking on any personal debt.	• Excellent. Only your money is at risk. • Don't put your personal financial and living expense requirements at risk. You will still have to eat and pay the mortgage.
Funded by a personal loan from a financial institution secured by personal assets.	• Are you going to be able to service this debt out of your new business? • Your security is now at risk should your business fail.
Funded by a personal loan from a financial institution with a personal guarantee.	• You are on the hook now. If your business fails, you will have to repay this debt personally.
Loan from an alternate source (a source other than a bank).	• You will usually pay higher interest rates and fees. • You will almost always have to provide a personal guarantee. • Will your business be able to make the payments on this loan commitment? • If you are unable to fulfill your commitments for repayment on this loan, what are the consequences?
Loan from a friend or family member.	• The absolute worst people to borrow money from are friends and family but unfortunately it can be unavoidable for many new entrepreneurs. • These loans should come with the same terms and conditions as if you were borrowing from a financial institution, including security and personal guarantees. • Make sure all paperwork is complete, legal, signed, and witnessed before any money changes hands. • If you are unable to fulfill your commitments for repayment of this loan, the resulting consequences can affect relationships forever. Money owing gives people an extremely long memory.

Here are some more topics to consider:

- Is there an opportunity for you to have some sales the day you start your business? It's possible, through your contacts and by putting in some extraordinary hours before your start-up day that you can secure a contract or two.

- Is this the right time to be starting your business? Timing is everything.

- Payment from your customers is always critical but during your first few months in business collecting payment from your customers on time may determine whether you survive.

- Do you know your costs for every aspect of the job you may be bidding on? If you don't know your costs, you can't produce an accurate and reliable job-cost estimate. It's that simple.

- Are there any extraordinary risks that you may be taking on with a specific project? For example:

  - Unacceptable payment terms.

  - The customer and/or general contractor are not financially sound.

  - You are unfamiliar with some aspects of the project scope.

  - Overall project management is sketchy, inexperienced, or nonexistent.

  - Your bid is too low.

  - The scope of the work is poorly defined.

  - The drawings and specifications are unclear.

  - You don't have all the necessary resources in place to undertake the project.

  - You have not taken into account extraordinary project conditions (e.g., weather, site conditions, travel time).

Small-business story

I was approached to become a partner in an established business that was somewhat related to my existing business. I agreed to become a partner with the current owner/manager. The business plan presented to me did not work out. Sales projections fell short by half. Needless to say this partnership did not last, but did not end until I had lost money.

Jack's response

If someone is offering you a business partnership, and you discover there is any risk involved, I would suggest that the contract be subject to sales targets being met. There may be an opportunity in a deal to agree to a period of time of three to six months where the seller must meet certain objectives and if the seller doesn't, the deal is off.

4

Meeting Your Customers' Objectives

Regardless of how you refer to your customers — they could be customers, clients, residents, patients, shoppers, subscribers, and students — no matter what they are called in your business they are your only source of sales revenue. For purposes of simplicity I will refer to this group as "customers" throughout the book.

What is a customer? A customer is a person or an organization that purchases goods and/or services from a store or business. Every one of us is a customer, and since we all have experience as customers, we certainly should know how customers want to be treated and how a business can earn customers' loyalty and respect. Take a minute to reflect on all of the businesses you deal with and the customer service you receive. Are you happy with every business where you shop? If you are not happy, do you have any ideas as to how these businesses could improve their customer service? I am sure every one of us has an opinion on this subject.

Customer service does not need to be some magical formula. There are some very basic things customers want and expect businesses to provide.

In my business I refer to all my customers' needs as objectives. When customers come to my business they are obviously in need of something and they expect me to be able to provide it. My job is to determine what my customers want and what their buying objectives are so I can meet their needs.

For example, when you go grocery shopping what are your objectives? You obviously want quality products; you don't want stale bread or sour milk. You want the food to be in the store and conveniently accessible. If you have questions, you want to deal with accessible, friendly, and well-informed staff. You want to pay a fair price or the lowest possible price, but you also want to receive good value for the money you are going to spend. You want a nice clean store to do your shopping; you are not going to shop in a dirty grocery store. You want the service at the checkout to be courteous and reasonably prompt. You want your groceries packed properly and in such a way to allow you to carry your groceries conveniently and safely. Finally, if you need assistance with your groceries, you expect the service to be considerate and helpful. If your grocery store can meet all of these objectives, you will probably return time and time again.

Another example would be your experience with restaurants. We all go to restaurants from time to time so we all have extensive experience in dealing with this type of business. Again, what are your objectives when you go to a restaurant? What you want may include a good location, great service, quality food and beverages, appropriate choices, clean premises, good value, and an atmosphere that meets your expectations for a particular establishment. If you have any special needs, you want those needs met as well.

Now, reflect on some of your best and worst restaurant experiences. In all of your best restaurant experiences, most likely all of your objectives were met — it is that simple. Regardless of whether it was a trip to McDonald's, a pizza shop, or the fanciest restaurant in town, the responsibility of the establishment is to meet all of your objectives. If it does that, you will return time and time again, you will build trust with the business, and you may build a relationship with the staff. One bad experience in a restaurant and you will likely never return, and you will probably tell all your friends about your bad experience as well. It is interesting to note that a bad experience is usually the result of one or two of your objectives not being met; it is highly unlikely that a functioning business would not meet any of your objectives. For example, if the service was bad but the food was good, what would you remember?

If the premises was dirty, what would you remember? If you felt you were overcharged, what would you remember?

Staying with the restaurant example a little longer, the basic customer objectives that must be met are quite simple:

- Location.

- Great service.

- Quality food and beverages.

- Appropriate choices.

- Clean premises.

- Good value.

- Great atmosphere.

- Special needs met.

Why do so many restaurants fail to meet their customers' objectives when there are only eight objectives that must be met? My guess is that the restaurant has not taken the time to really understand its customers' objectives and it has failed to train the staff properly; therefore, bad management.

Small-business story: Restauranteur

I had been in the restaurant and hotel business for more than 30 years but I had always worked for someone else. I figured I knew everything there was to know in this business so I decided to open my own restaurant and move back to the city where I worked and lived for many years. I found what I believed to be a great location where a restaurant was located previously; therefore, my capital expenditures to get started were reasonable. Now it was opening day.

Customer

I knew the proprietor from his previous time in our city so we decided to patronize his business on opening day; we wanted to do everything we could do to support this new business. When we were walking in we met friends walking out. They said, "Don't go in; it's terrible." I said, "I know the owner; it can't be that bad." Guess what? It was terrible! The service was slow or nonexistent, the food was terrible, and the atmosphere was poor. Other than these three objectives not being met, everything else was okay. We never went back.

Restauranteur

I don't know what I did wrong but my business failed within two months and I lost my life's savings. I thought I knew the business, but I guess not. I packed up and left town for good. My creditors chased me for more than a year and then finally gave up. This was an extremely stressful experience and it had a devastating impact on me and my family.

Jack's response

It has been said that if you want to make a small fortune in the restaurant business, you should start with a large fortune. This isn't always true because there are many successful restaurants and restauranteurs. It is a tough business, but the restaurants that are successful are doing a great job of meeting their customers' objectives and building trust and relationships with them. If you fail to meet one of your customer's objectives, you are putting your business at risk and you may fail. Meet all of your customers' objectives every time and you will give your business the best possible chance of succeeding.

Your customers all have buying objectives that they want met. If you want to have successful and profitable relationships with your customers, you must know what their objectives are and then you must meet them. Customers have choices as to who they will do business with because in almost every industry there is a lot of competition. What you want is to be the preferred supplier or preferred business in your customers' opinion. This relationship starts with you knowing and understanding what your customers' objectives are.

In some businesses, customers' objectives can be quite basic. Even in the complex restaurant business there are only seven primary customer objectives (plus any special needs). In the construction/trades business, the industry, all of the customers' project objectives fall into the categories of Faster, Cheaper, Better. In some more complex industries, the list of customer objectives may be much longer. The bottom line is that you must know and understand your customers' objectives in order to meet their needs.

For example, in the construction/trades industry, if you have fully documented a specific customer's objectives in the areas of quality (Better) and price (Cheaper) but you failed to understand and/or document your customer's schedule (Faster) objectives, you have set yourself up to fail. You may meet your customer's quality objectives and price objectives, but if you failed to meet its schedule objectives, the entire project, in the customer's opinion, may be a disaster.

A simple example would be if you built a venue for a wedding and you did a great job on the quality and price, but you were a day late and didn't complete the project until the day after the wedding. Obviously your customer is not going to be happy. So why didn't you know what the project schedule was? Did you not ask your customer? It is your responsibility to know, understand, and document your customer's objectives, then present a plan that will meet all of those needs. The next step is to execute your plan and still meet your customer's objectives.

Take for example a shoe salesperson. I really like this example because if your objectives are not met when you go to buy a pair of shoes, you are not going to be happy. What are your objectives when you go to buy a pair of shoes — style, fit, comfort, price, service, and availability? You know your objectives, but how is the shoe salesperson going to know your objectives unless he or she asks and then understands your objectives? If you are dealing with a true professional, he or she will know how to get you to share your objectives and then the salesperson will put the effort into meeting your objectives.

Think of the experience: You were greeted when you walked into the shoe store in a professional and noninvasive style by the sales representative beginning a conversation and within a few minutes, he or she learned of all of your objectives. The salesperson then provided you with a range of options that he or she believed would meet your objectives; after a few trials and a few options, all of your objectives were zeroed in on. When you made your final choice, the sales professional reviewed your objectives to ensure that all of your objectives were fully met; you paid for your purchase and left as a very satisfied customer. The next day you posted on Facebook how great your buying experience was. That shoe salesperson is going to be very successful in his or her career.

By now you should be getting the idea that in your business all your customers want is to have their buying objectives met. By meeting your customers' buying objectives each and every time, you will be well on your way to creating trust with your customers and cementing long-term relationships with repeat customers. What else could any business ask for?

What happens if you can't meet a customer's buying objectives? The truth is you can't be everything to every customer and you can't meet every customer's objectives every time. There are some customers who would be better off doing business with your competitors. There is nothing wrong with this. You can't have and you don't want all of the customers; you want customers that will ensure that you can meet your objectives as well.

Here are your objectives for your customers:

- A customer must provide the opportunity for your business to profit from the relationship.

- When there is an opportunity for repeat business, you want to establish a level of trust with the customer in order to build a lasting relationship.

- You want your customer to spread the word about how good your business is. Note that word-of-mouth advertising is the best form of advertising and it's free!

Now you should ask yourself: How do I ensure that my business objectives are met? This is easy. Just meet your customers' buying objectives every time and only deal with customers that will allow you to meet your business objectives. Voila! You are on your way to building a successful business.

Small-business story

At one time, in a major industry in North America, the number one salesperson in the organization sold twice as much as the number two salesperson. How is this possible in a very competitive field with thousands of sales personnel (who were all employed by numerous small-business franchisees)?

Jack's response

Obviously this person was an extremely good sales representative who must have relied on repeat business. I would bet that every one of the customers had their buying objectives met and, over a period of time, the majority of the sales were earned by repeat business from customers who had a trusting and respectful relationship with their sales representative.

Every small business is unique and the culture within the business is almost always established by the business owners. Small-business culture is typically created by the owner's work ethic, established business objectives, policies and procedures, the industry the business is in, and the employees who support the business. Creating a culture within your business of *always meeting your customers' buying objectives* is the primary foundation of every successful small business. Therefore, if you want to be successful, you need to adopt this policy, create this culture within your business, and ensure your partners and employees all buy into it.

Sounds simple though doesn't it? All we have to do is meet our customers' objectives every time! Easy to say, but not easy to do. Here are some guidelines on how to accomplish this simple yet complex task:

- You must learn from your customers and/or business experience what your customers' buying objectives are for your particular business and/or industry.

- You need to communicate with your customers in order to determine what their objectives are. Note that in some industries those objectives can be forever changing.

- If you don't know or understand your customers' buying objectives, you won't be able to meet their objectives.

- Once customers' objectives are known and/or established in your company you need to have in place what is necessary to ensure that the customers' objectives can be met.

- You need to build within your organization a culture of commitment to meeting your customers' objectives and the culture of commitment must be prevalent from the top to the bottom of the organization.

A CEO's big-business story

We have a policy in our company: We don't talk to our customers and our customers don't talk to us.

Jack's response

This was a large and long-established company that went bankrupt because it no longer understood its customers' buying needs so therefore it was not meeting its customers' buying objectives.

5
Faster, Cheaper, Better

Every customer has only three project objectives and they are Faster, Cheaper, Better. Contractors have been telling their customers for years that they do three kinds of jobs: quick jobs, cheap jobs, and good jobs and you can have any *two* that you want:

- A quick, good job isn't going to be cheap.
- A quick, cheap job isn't going to be good.
- A cheap, good job isn't going to be fast.

What if your customer doesn't want to choose just two out of the three objectives? It seems logical that your customer wants all three: quick, good, and cheap, or said another way, Faster, Cheaper, Better. As an extraordinary business, you can deliver Faster, Cheaper, Better jobs.

We are not saying Fastest, Cheapest, Best; we are saying by comparison Faster, Cheaper, Better. That when compared to your competitors your services as a whole will be Faster, Cheaper, Better than your competitors. You may not always be the *Fastest*; you may not always be the *Cheapest*; you may not always be the *Best* in all aspects of the project, but taken as a whole on a project, you will be Faster, Cheaper, Better when compared to any of your competition.

This is what Faster, Cheaper, Better means to a contractor:

- **Faster:** Always on schedule or ahead of schedule.

- **Cheaper:** Always competitive and providing the customer with good value.

- **Better:** Always a quality installation and a better project process.

Now here is something that is most interesting. Every customer project objective that you identify and/or document will fall under one of the three categories of Faster, Cheaper, Better. What does this mean? There will be a number of documented project objectives but in every case every one of the defined project objectives will fall under one of the primary objectives of Faster, Cheaper, Better.

If we were to take a sample project and have six contractors complete the exact same project, we know that one of the contractors will complete the project first, one contractor will complete the project for the least amount of money, and one contractor will have the best quality and project process. It's unlikely that one of the contractors will be number one in all three categories. But what if one of the contractors was rated as the contractor that was overall Faster, Cheaper, and Better when compared to the other five contractors? Wouldn't that be the contractor that is the real hands-down winner?

The contractor who finished the project first may have incurred higher costs, so did his project quality and process suffer?

The contractor who finished the project at the lowest cost may have missed the scheduled completion date, so did her project quality and process suffer?

The contractor who had the best quality and project process may have missed the scheduled completion date, so did he incur higher costs?

Then there was the contractor who was rated overall as the best contractor when all three categories were taken into account. This contractor was overall Faster, Cheaper, Better when compared to all of the other contractors! That's the contractor the customer wants to do business with because he is likely the only contractor who met all of the project objectives of the customer.

Was he the Fastest? No. But the project was completed on or ahead of schedule.

Was he the Cheapest? No. But the project was on or under budget and the customer was provided with very good value for every project dollar spent.

Was he the Best in quality and project process? No. But the customer was provided with a job that met all of the customer's quality objectives and the project process was seamless and trouble-free for the customer.

As you can appreciate, this is an extremely important concept. Exactly what does Faster, Cheaper, Better mean and how do you achieve Faster, Cheaper, Better on every one of your projects? Let's define Faster, Cheaper, Better.

Small-business story

We had a long and successful relationship with a very good customer. We always met our customer's objectives and as a consequence the customer continued to provide us with more business, more complex projects, and much larger projects. Our customer was considering us for a major out-of-state project and based on our long-term relationship the customer selected us for the project. You can imagine how upset the local contractors were when the contract was awarded to an out-of-state small business. Those are the rewards of meeting a customer's project objectives every time out!

1. Faster

You complete all of your project responsibilities right on schedule. This means not a day late and not ahead of schedule if you are going to incur additional costs (earlier is okay if you are not going to incur additional costs). The customer said "be done on a certain day" and on that day you were 100 percent complete, not 99 percent complete, but 100 percent complete. What else could the customer ask for? Cheaper and Better of course!

2. Cheaper

You provide your customer with excellent value for every project dollar he or she spends with you. Yes, you expect to make a fair profit on the services you provide and the customer expects this. What the customer wants to know is that every dollar he or she spends with your company is going to provide him or her with excellent value. What else could the customer ask for? Better, of course.

3. Better

Better doesn't refer to just the quality of the installation. To the customer, a Better project means the overall project experience from beginning to end and the quality of the installation. A Better journey for the customer throughout the entire project! A project where the customer enjoys a trouble-free relationship with the contractor in which communication by the contractor is efficient, effective, and timely, and the contractor is committed to meeting the customer's project objectives. The end result is a quality installation.

4. Good Project Management Will Help You Achieve Faster, Cheaper, Better

How is Faster, Cheaper, Better achieved? One way, and one way only — excellent project management! Project management is the management of the project process from beginning to end; once the project has been sold to the customer and you are ready to build it for less than you sold it for. The project process starts and continues until the project is 100 percent complete and full payment has been received from the customer.

Is project management mandatory? No. At the end of the day the light switch will still turn on the light on a poorly managed project just as it will on a well-managed project. The difference between a well-managed project and a poorly managed project is that on a well-managed project Faster, Cheaper, Better will be achieved and a poorly managed project will likely be behind schedule, incur more costs, and the project process journey could be a disaster.

5. Managing the Project Process

A project is a task or group of tasks that are completed within a defined starting time or date and a defined finish time or date. The project process is what takes place between the project start date and the project completion date. You complete a number of projects everyday throughout your life. For example, today I am going to the grocery store so I get in my car, drive to the store, shop, return home, and put the groceries away. The project started when I decided to go to the grocery store and the project ended when I put the groceries away. Was there a management component to this project?

An unmanaged trip to the grocery store does not involve a preplan; it only involves the actual return trip and shopping. A managed trip to the grocery store likely involves the following process:

1. Make a list.

2. Check with your spouse or partner to see if he or she would like to add anything to the list.

3. Plan your trip to coincide with other projects that you may have to complete at the same time.

4. Plan your trip at a time that is convenient for you and when the store is not busy.

5. Stay on track and stick to the list by checking off the items as you put them in your basket.

6. Organize the groceries at the checkout in the best order for putting them away at home.

7. Return home.

8. Put the groceries away.

Here's the difference between a managed trip to the grocery store and an unmanaged trip to the grocery store:

- The managed trip likely took less time, therefore it was Faster.

- The managed trip had a list and you stuck to it, so your shopping trip was Cheaper.

- The managed trip avoided the rush hour and you didn't forget anything, so the entire process was Better.

Therefore, a project as simple as going to the grocery store, if properly managed, will result in a Faster, Cheaper, Better shopping experience.

Now, I am not suggesting that you want to apply Faster, Cheaper, Better to every aspect of your life. You may end up driving your spouse or partner crazy. What I am saying is that in business every project process needs to be managed in order to produce Faster, Cheaper, Better results. Your customer is paying the bill so he or she wants Faster, Cheaper, Better, which means project management shouldn't be optional in your business. You need to manage every project you undertake.

Before determining how to best manage projects in your business, let's look at the fundamental field components of every project. Whether you are doing the field work yourself or you hire field personnel, you need to provide the following on-site for each and every project if you hope to achieve Faster, Cheaper, Better results:

- You need the material for the project readily available on-site when required.

- You need the tools and equipment necessary for the project, all in good repair, and readily available on-site when it is required.

- You need the skilled labor on-site capable of undertaking the project tasks when required.

- One person should be assigned to lead the project process on-site.

- You need to provide clear and concise information (e.g., plans, specifications, drawings, scope, customer's project objectives) to the project personnel that clearly define the scope of the work. Information should be reduced to bite-sized pieces and not in overwhelming package sizes.

- Project personnel need to be provided with clear and concise direction as to what the project expectations are (e.g., schedule, budget, project quality).

That's really all you need to do for the site personnel to do their jobs efficiently and effectively. In my experience, on well-managed projects, your typical poorer performers will perform at the level of your best performers. By managing all of the above processes you have just taken away any excuse your poorer workers could have to perform poorly. You have just made their jobs easy and no one on-site has any excuse but to work up to your performance expectations. Now if you let the site down and mismanage any aspect of the on-site processes, your poor performers will typically make a mess of things, whereas your good performers will try to work around your mismanagement and still get the job done.

The bottom line is if you fail to manage all the on-site required processes, you will not achieve Faster, Cheaper, Better and you won't meet your customer's project objectives. On every project, at some point in time, you are going to have to provide the necessary project elements defined in this chapter, and throughout this book. Why not do it with good project management?

Small-business story

We did a fabulous job for our customer; or so I thought. We met all of his objectives as far as I was concerned. When the project was completed, Faster, Cheaper, Better in my opinion, the customer pointed out that I had supplied one piece of used equipment. This was always my intention and I am sure I told the customer verbally that this one piece of equipment would be used due to the cost of price and delivery of a new piece of equipment but unfortunately the contract did not state that this piece of equipment was going to be used. The customer demanded a substantial credit and I had to comply if I wanted to do business with him again. From now on I will make sure that whatever I am going to provide will be clearly stated in writing, not in verbal terms. As the saying goes, "verbal orders are lost in space"!

6
Sales

If you don't have sales, you don't have a business. Just ask any of the entrepreneurs on the TV shows *Dragons' Den* or *Shark Tank*. The easiest thing to do in the business world is to set up a business. I could go out tomorrow and lease some space, buy some products, get a business license, put up a sign, and set up shop selling whatever. Will I be successful? Only if I can make enough sales to make my business profitable.

Lack of sales is probably the biggest reason for most business failures. You can have everything in place in your business for production, operations, inventory, accounting, finance, and administration but if you don't have sales, your business will fail. Typically you have total control over everything in your business; however, your customers will determine your fate in the sales department.

If you listen to various business reports, they will always be talking about sales, sales growth, new product sales, year-over-year increases in sales, and sales plans. This should give you an idea of just how important sales are to a business. Large businesses and most small businesses are always looking for ways to increase sales and grow their businesses.

Successful salespeople are hard to define. Why is this person so successful at sales and this other person isn't, but they both seem equal to the task? In my career, trying to figure out why a particular person is good at sales while another person isn't has always been a challenge. Take for example the real estate business, where in some agencies 20 percent of the agents earn 80 percent of the commissions and the remaining 80 percent of the agents fight over the remaining 20 percent. How is this possible? I don't believe there is any magic formula but I do believe there are some common traits amongst successful salespeople:

- **Customer trust:** The customers trust the salesperson they are dealing with and the salesperson, through whatever means, earns that trust.

- **Product knowledge:** The salesperson demonstrates excellent product knowledge.

- **Buying objectives understood:** The salesperson has the ability and takes the time to learn what the customers' buying objectives are.

- **Buying objectives met:** The salesperson is able to demonstrate to the customers and then convince the customers that their buying objectives will be met.

- **Reliable:** The salesperson proves he or she is reliable by calling customers back when he or she has promised to do so. The salesperson fulfils commitments by providing information at a certain time and date.

- **Ability to close:** The salesperson has the ability to close the deal with the customers.

- **Follow up:** The salesperson stays involved in the transaction to ensure all of the seller's commitments are fulfilled and the buyer's objectives are met.

Over the last few decades the role of the salesperson has greatly diminished in some industries. For example, in most big-box stores and mass retailers the salesperson is virtually nonexistent. Their sales strategy is to get you into their store where you will self-shop for the most part. In small businesses this is not the case because they are typically reliant on their ability and the ability of their sales staff to sell and meet their defined sales targets.

Big-business story

Target failed in its plans to enter the Canadian retail market. It spent millions of dollars acquiring leases and doing leasehold improvements as well as setting up shop in many Canadian cities. Within two years the Canadian operations had filed for bankruptcy and the accumulated losses over the two-year period exceeded $2 billion.

Jack's response

Target Canada failed to meet its customers' buying objectives. Canadian customers had expectations that the Canadian Target stores would be the same as the American stores and this was not the case. The customers' buying objectives were not met so the consumers did not support Target. Its sales objectives were not met so the business failed.

You may find it hard to believe that a large successful company such as Target could fail in such a huge business venture, but it did. It had control over all aspects of its business plan except for sales. When projected sales failed to materialize the company failed.

What should Target have done? Business experts around the world will be writing about this for years to come. Target's move into Canada, a market it was not familiar with, was far too aggressive. Its sales targets were based on wishful thinking and not on proven business data. Most importantly, it failed to meet the customers' buying objectives.

What happened to the executives who were behind this monumental failure? Some may have lost their jobs, some may have been demoted, and some may have been encouraged to retire. Did any of them lose a lot of personal money? No. However, if this had been a small-business venture, the business owners and investors would likely have lost all of their investment and, in some cases, may have faced personal bankruptcy. That, in itself, is one of the huge differences between big business and small business. Small-business entrepreneurs risk it all, while big-business owners don't.

1. Can You Sell?

There are three parts to every business — sell, produce, and account. You should be extremely adept at two out of three of these skills and have a good working knowledge of the third. Are you a salesperson or can you train yourself to be one? If you can't sell, you will need to hire and rely on employees to fulfil this task. Without adequate sales every business will ultimately fail.

The following is a sampling of the small-business sector:

- **Retail** : In retail the sales personnel are the front persons for the entire business. If the business is small with one location, then the small-business entrepreneur will likely play an active role in selling.

- **Service industry:** In the service industry the small-business entrepreneur may be directly involved in the provision of services to customers. In this industry, word-of-mouth advertising is the key source for bringing in new customers and creating customer loyalty, which leads to repeat sales.

- **Restaurants:** In the restaurant industry getting customers in the door is key. Once a customer enters your business you can assume that he or she will be spending money and you will be making a sale. The sales process starts as soon as the customer walks in the door and the server is on the frontline of ensuring the sale goes well and the customer's objectives are met. Just like the service industry, word-of-mouth advertising is the key source of new customers and customer loyalty.

- **Professional services:** In this industry (e.g., chiropractors, opticians, legal services, consultants) customers are buying a service that is typically complex and not necessarily fully understood by the consumer; that is why the service is provided by a professional. The professional, if he or she wants to be successful, still has the same obligations to his or her customers. The basic rules still apply. The buyer's objectives must be understood and met.

- **Manufacturers:** A typical small-business manufacturing plant has a fixed maximum capacity. If the plant can consistently sell out its entire production and operate at 100 percent capacity, the business has a very good chance of success.

- **Construction:** The construction industry is driven by small business. Every community has an electrical contractor, plumber, painter, builder, etc., and they are usually small businesses. This sector needs to provide Faster, Cheaper, Better services in order to be successful and meet sales objectives.

Small-business story

I wanted to set up my own small business and become an entrepreneur. I looked around our community and other communities and I came upon a franchise business in the specialty food sector (ice cream). I looked into the business further and without a lot of research I plowed ahead and signed an agreement. I signed a three-year lease with the landlord that I had to personally guarantee because of the lack of net worth in my business.

Working with the franchisor I wrote a business plan and set my sales targets. The franchisor was able to help me with the cost of sales and expense sections of my business plan but I was primarily responsible for setting the sales targets.

Opening day was great as we did extensive advertising leading up to the day. For the first month sales were great and we actually exceeded our sales targets but then sales went flat and month after month we did not meet our sales targets. This was like dying a slow death. Month after month the business was losing money and bleeding me dry. I tried everything that I could afford to increase sales to no avail. Our sales stayed steady but were not enough to sustain the business and make a profit.

I talked to my landlord about my situation but he was not sympathetic. I talked to the franchisor and it tried to help me to increase sales again to no avail. I tried to sell the business and I actually advertised it for sale but once prospective buyers understood my situation they just walked away.

In the end I had to hang on to the business until my lease expired. The day my lease expired I was out of there. I salvaged whatever I could and that was the end of my business. Five years later I finally paid off all debts that I had incurred in the business. This business experience took its toll on me and my family and in the end it was a valuable experience. Unfortunately I just don't have the gumption to try another business so I will stay an employee for the rest of my career. I do have a newfound respect though for all small-business entrepreneurs, especially those who are successful.

Jack's response

This particular situation has happened to many aspiring small-business entrepreneurs. It looks like this was a case of "management by wishful thinking" when it came to setting the sales targets in the business plan. One more example of how lack of sales will kill a business.

2. Top Ten Ways to Sell Your Product and/or Service

Where do sales and customers come from? How do customers learn about your business? The following sections discuss the top ten ways to sell your product and/or service.

2.1 Repeat business

In every business there is a cost to attract a new customer; for some businesses it could be thousands of dollars to attract one new customer. There is no cost to acquiring repeat business. Repeat customers come to your business or contact your business because they have a need. Often a business's repeat customers won't even contact the competition. You can't ask for anything better than that. If you are a start-up business, you won't have any repeat business on day one but if you look after your customers and meet all of their buying objectives, repeat business may be a significant part of your business before too long.

Small-business story

I have always wanted to be a small-business entrepreneur. I worked for many years in our family business and for my uncle's business. Although I had no interest in carrying on in the family business I was determined to have my own one day. I was continually looking for opportunities and when an opportunity was presented I would thoroughly research the business and prepare a preliminary business plan. I had studied business in college so putting together a business plan was no problem for me.

Nothing appealed to me until one day a business came up for sale and I was asked if I was interested. Again I did a preliminary business plan and the business looked promising. The cost to get into the business was $100,000 which I did not have, but through savings, remortgaging my home, and borrowing from relatives and from our local small-business bank I was able to raise the required funds.

I have been in business for five years. Although I have faced many challenges along the way, my business has been a success. My primary focus in the business is sales. I have a great installation crew who can look after the installation side of my business (under my supervision) but I take full responsibility for meeting my sales objectives. In my business word-of-mouth, repeat business, and great relationships with my customers have allowed me to meet my sales targets every year. I would like to grow my business one day but for now I really want to focus on doing what I know best and doing lots of it. This motto has worked for me very well so far.

2.2 Social media and word of mouth

Social media and word of mouth have merged over the past few years. There is still word of mouth but the words, for the most part, are expressed on social media. There are still many conversations that take place in person; for example, if someone has had a good or bad experience with a business, the subject will almost always come up. If your business is consistently meeting the customers' buying objectives, everything that will be said by word of mouth or social media will be positive and you couldn't ask for any better advertising than that. The best part is that it's free!

2.3 Referrals

Referrals are related to word of mouth but are more specific where a potential customer is asking someone where to buy something or where to get a service and your business is referred or recommended. The person doing the referring may be a customer of yours or heard good things about your business but the referral will be positive as the person giving it is putting his or her reputation on the line.

2.4 Websites

Almost every business today has a website. There are two key things to websites: One, if potential customers search the Internet for a particular subject, will they be referred to your website? Will your website pop up? Two, when potential customers arrive at your website will they find the information they are looking for in a readable and informative format?

If you have a poorly designed website, you may be better off with no website at all. An informative website that easily guides potential customers to the information they want is invaluable. Having your website pop up during a search is a far greater challenge that you will need to address with your website developer.

2.5 Personal sales calls

The art of the personal sales call to a customer is not dead even though there are so many other options to communicate with customers today. Personal calls can be by telephone, in person, or even by email. The point is that it is a personal connection between you or your sales representative and a customer. Everyone still loves that personal care and attention and it is the basis for building long-term relationships with customers which is the foundation of repeat business.

2.6 Advertising

Advertising comes in all different shapes and sizes, choices and options, types and forms. A wise person once said, "Half the money I spend on advertising works; the only problem is I don't know which half works and which half doesn't." That is the way advertising goes. Take a look around at all the advertising businesses do in your community.

Big businesses do major advertising campaigns on television, in newspapers, and in magazines. For example, a 30-second spot during the Super Bowl costs about $4 million. That is a lot of money for any business, but for some large businesses this type of advertising works. For small businesses this is not an option. Typically for a small business, advertising dollars are focused on local print media, radio, local TV, Yellow Pages, and other local advertising opportunities. There can be a substantial cost to this type of advertising and every business should closely monitor the costs and benefits related to advertising. You should try to make your advertising dollars be 100 percent effective; not 50 percent effective.

2.7 Community involvement and special events

There is a full range of options when it comes to community involvement and special events. This type of promotion can be tied to service clubs, professional organizations, business associations, charities, and community and sporting events. Being a good corporate citizen in your community is a great foundation for positive word of mouth and referrals.

2.8 Agencies

Some businesses may enlist the services of a third party to promote and sell their products and services. Agents, who may represent a full range of related products and services (but ideally not your competitors), can provide much broader exposure for your business as the agents can typically book orders directly with your company. Remember that all agents and agencies are not created equal and you want to be sure that the time and effort you spend in setting up these types of relationships pay off for your business. Make sure you do thorough research, check references, set and agree on targets, and train your agents before turning them loose on your customers.

2.9 Sales staff

Your business may warrant your own sales staff. For example, automobile sales and real estate firms employ their own sales forces and without them there likely wouldn't be any sales at all. Successful businesses attract the best sales personnel and they need to be compensated accordingly. In every business your salespeople are the ones who will have the first contact and interaction with your customers. You never get a second chance to make a first impression so you want to make sure you employ the best in these positions and that your sales force is well trained and fully committed to your business, your products, and your services. Most importantly, they should be dedicated to you, the small-business entrepreneur, who employs them.

2.10 Responding to customer requests

Many customers, especially government agencies, will issue requests for suppliers to respond with proposals and pricing for a specific service or project. This is very common in the construction industry. A customer-issued request is often referred to as a Request for Proposal (RFP), Request for Quotation (RFQ), or Request for Information (RFI). The bidding criteria for you and your competitors is intended to be level in these cases.

So far we have talked about customers and how to make sales. The biggest question is: What sales volume are you going to project for your small business? If you work backwards and create a business plan based on how you envision your business will be structured, you will quickly determine that you need a specific level of sales in order for your business to be successful and profitable. If you work in logical order and determine your potential sales volume based on sales data for your area, market share, business activity, and the economy, you will need to build your business around the sales projections for your company. Every business must have a business plan with sales projections, ideally projected for a five-year period going forward. No matter where you set your sales targets, you need to know that if you fail to meet those targets, your business is going to be in trouble or you will have to rethink your entire plan. No matter where you set your sales targets, whether they be $100,000, $1 million, or $10 million, you must base the targets on realistic achievable goals and then these targets must be achieved.

Small-business story

We set our sales target for this year at $11 million. Last year we did $10 million so projecting a 10 percent increase for this year seemed reasonable and achievable. We are going into our new fiscal year with 30 percent of the year's business in hand so we should be in great shape.

During the year we were presented with what we thought were great business opportunities and we pursued every one. We determined that we could handle the extra business. Unfortunately this was not the case. We did $20 million in business and made less money than if we just made our $11 million budget. We had problems with capacity, employees, cash flow, receivables, payables, and administration, just to name a few. Our trip into Small-Business Hell relates to too much business and not to a shortage of business. We now know that sales targets must be met and may be reasonably exceeded but trying to do twice as much business as our business plan called for put our entire business in jeopardy. We have learned a valuable lesson and future business plans will take into account a cap or maximum amount of sales growth that we can handle in a year. On the positive side, we now know about the pitfalls of growing too fast and as we move forward with our five-year business plan projections, we will be much more realistic.

Jack's response

Yes it is possible to have too much business. Too much business may stretch your business to the breaking point, put unbearable pressure on you as a small-business entrepreneur, and overtax your working capital and your ability to finance your business. We all enjoy business growth but it must provide an opportunity for the business to be more profitable and not put the business at risk.

7

The Importance of Quality Products and Services

A fundamental of business is that you have to sell your goods and/or services for more than your cost and with adequate margins to ensure your business can operate profitably. For example, if you are selling widgets for $10 and your cost for each widget is $5 then you have a $5 margin on every widget you sell. If you have a sales target of $1 million, you are projecting to sell 100,000 widgets. What if your competitor is also selling widgets that are just as good as yours but it is buying the widgets for $4 marking them up $5 and selling them for $9? Your competitor's margin is the same as yours but he has a lower selling price. Assuming all other things being equal in the marketplace, your business will be at a distinct disadvantage. So what are you going to do about it?

In business if you are reselling anything, your cost for the goods has to be at least as good as what your competitor can buy them for. If you are really good at business, you will be buying at less than your competition and you will be in the preferred position in the marketplace.

This is a basic example but the message here is that if you are going to sell anything to customers, and you expect to make a reasonable margin for overhead and profit, you have to make sure that you have the lowest possible cost base. In the service industry, you can't deliver on the customers' buying objectives of Faster, Cheaper, Better if your competitor has a competitive advantage over you.

I have to assume that you know your business, industry, and the supply chain process that gets goods to your door ready for resale. There is quite often a significant and sometimes complex supply chain providing your business with goods. It is imperative that you understand this process and where you fit into the supply chain. Then and only then can you be assured that you are buying the goods that you are planning to resell at the best possible price.

There is no upside to buying inferior products at a lesser price and trying to pawn them off at a higher selling price. Consumers are way too savvy for those tricks of the trade. You know your objective is to meet your customer's buying objectives, and making sure that you are doing everything you can to get the competitive advantage over your competitors is a really good start.

The question that you must be constantly asking yourself is: "How can I reduce the costs of goods that I will be reselling while still meeting my customers' buying objectives?" Then, take appropriate action to achieve this objective. Consider the following to achieve your objective:

- Understand the supply chain for the goods that you are reselling to ensure that you are buying at the best possible price.

- Build relationships and trust with suppliers that result in you getting the benefit of the best possible price.

- Buy direct or higher up the supply chain than your competitors to eliminate the middleperson, which will allow you to buy at a lower cost.

- Be the customer that your supplier wants to do business with because you are organized, professional, and know how to deal with the supplier's sales protocols.

- Buy in bulk where appropriate but never allow yourself to be stuck with stale, nonmoving inventory.

- Participate in buying groups in your industry, if they will provide you with a competitive advantage.

- Negotiate payment terms that meet your requirements but always explore options that could provide you with a competitive advantage.

If you are only providing a service that does not involve the resale of any goods or products, then the above doesn't necessarily apply to your business. The question is, who is going to provide the service to your customers? If you are using employees to provide services or installations to your customers, you are dealing with all employee-related matters. The employee/employer relationship is so important I have dedicated Chapter 8 just to employees so this will be covered there.

Small-business story

I invented an installation system that I believed would deliver Faster, Cheaper, Better installations to my customers. The system was definitely Faster to install and commission. The end result was Cheaper. But the system ultimately had quality problems and quickly proved to not be Better. In this case two out of three was not good enough and my invention quickly became a thing of the past. Did this mistake throw me into Small-Business Hell? Temporarily yes, but I fought my way out as fast as I could.

1. Make Your Brand Recognizable

What are you going to sell or what service do you sell in your business? Do your customers know and understand what you do and the services and, or things they could buy from your business? If you have a small business, or you are planning to start one, you must be selling or planning on selling something to your customers such as the following:

- Products
- Services
- Installations

Whatever it is you are selling your business name will be associated with what you do. We all know what the following major corporations do:

- Walmart
- McDonald's
- GM

- Boeing

- Apple

- Visa

- Best Buy

- Century 21

- United Airlines

- Walgreens

If you want to buy an airplane, you wouldn't go to McDonald's. If you needed a new computer, you wouldn't go to Century 21. Name association to a business's products and services is critical — whether it is a big or small business. Big corporations have us well trained so we know what they are selling. The small-business sector needs to be more definitive.

Your small business needs to be known for the products and services you provide. Any one of the following could be a small business in your community and every one of these businesses is identifiable by its name:

- Coldstream Plumbing and Heating

- Springfield Ladies' Wear

- Smith's Pharmacy

- ABC Taxi

- West Bend Flower Shop

- Jones Legal Services

- Majestic Home Builders

- Beaumont RV Sales

- North River Mortgage Brokers

- Jay's Sandwich Shop

Consider the name of your business and make sure customers know what you do so you can meet their buying objectives.

8
Employees

Unless you are planning on doing all the work yourself in your business, or with only your partners, you are going to need employees. In large businesses, employees are the face of the entire business. For example, Walmart employs 2.1 million people (www.businessinsider.com/walmart-employees-pay, accessed October, 2015). Now that is a large workforce. In small businesses, the workforces are much smaller; typically anywhere from 1 to 100 employees. Regardless of how many workers you have, your obligations to your employees are the same.

Whether you have a written agreement with an employee or not you are obligated by law to certain terms and conditions that must be adhered to in your business. Employment law varies throughout North America so do your research on labor laws in your area. This chapter will focus on the relationship between the employee and the employer.

Employer, boss, company — no matter what your organization is defined as, or how it is referred to, if you have employees, then those employees have been hired for a specific reason and to perform specific tasks for your small business.

Small-business story

I hired a CFO (chief financial officer) for my small business as I wanted my business to really grow. In fact, I hired my CFO out of a large public company. He came with big ideas and big credentials but unfortunately he did not fit the small-business mold. He pushed me and prodded me into business deals that I should never have considered. When my business got into trouble, primarily based on his bad advice, the new CFO left and I was in Small-Business Hell.

Jack's response

Most small businesses need to manage our businesses as small businesses even if we are doing millions of dollars in sales. Therefore key employees need to think like small-business entrepreneurs and not lead us into business deals that are not right for our businesses. A well-thought-out business plan should identify the needs and skills for a CFO in a growing small business.

In small business, you or one of your managers will be responsible for hiring employees. The hiring process is critical in every business but especially in small businesses. If you are a sole proprietor operating as a small-business entrepreneur, and you employ ten people, the majority of the tasks in your company are going to be taken on and be the responsibility of employees. If you want your business to be successful, you will want to hire the best employees that you can attract to your business.

If you have more than a few employees, you may rely on some employees more than others. For example, you may have managers or assistant managers — people who are typically referred to as key employees. There are many large and small businesses where the business relies on key employees to manage and operate various aspects of the business. Development of key employees is critical for growing businesses that want to succeed. The following are some traits that you should look for in potential key employees:

- Respect, admiration, and commitment to you as their employer. You would never want to rely on a person who is not committed to the success of your business.

- Trained, qualified, and educated for their position of responsibility today and tomorrow.

- Team players.

- A person who earns and deserves respect from other people in the organization. You don't want to promote someone in your business who is not respected by other employees.

- A person who earns respect from customers.

- A leader.

- Trustworthy.

- Communicative.

- Reliable.

There are many more traits that you may look for in key employees that are applicable to your business. Successful small-business entrepreneurs know how to pick and groom key employees for their businesses.

Small-business story

I had a key employee who I believed was going to work his way up to partner in my business. One day I asked this employee to give me a report on his department and how we could improve service, lower cost, and improve quality. A day later he handed me a one-page report that basically said "hire more people." He was let go a month later. You cannot build the A Team with B Team players.

1. Preparing a Job Description

When contemplating hiring an employee, create a detailed job description with all of the employee's qualifications and requirements listed. Sample 4 is an example for a bookkeeper position in a small business with 25 employees. If there is more than one manager or small-business owner involved in the decision, make sure that everyone is in agreement with the job description as this will form the basis for the hiring process for this employee and ultimately the employment agreement. Also, agree on a hiring committee or agree that one person will take responsibility for hiring this employee. See Sample 4 for an example of a job description and duties.

Preparing a detailed job description it provides the employer with the opportunity to clearly state the objectives of the position and define what duties are expected of the employee.

Once you have prepared the job description and you are satisfied with it, you can create the posting for the position that could be advertised, and posted internally and externally. See Sample 5.

Job Description and Duties

Bookkeeper Position with ABC Company

Job Description and Duties

Customer Liaison: Although customer liaison and contact are not a significant part of this position, everyone employed at ABC must retain a good relationship with all customers and must enjoy working with customers.

Supplier Orders: Work with other departments to assist with supplier orders and accounts.

Payroll: Handle all aspects of payroll including receipt of time sheets, approval of time sheets by manager, entering payroll, preparing checks, and managing deductions and remittances.

Invoicing and Accounts Receivable: Issue invoices for all provided services and collect accounts receivable.

Payables: Record, file, obtain manager approval, and prepare checks for all payables. Look after all supplier accounts as required.

Banking: Look after all bank deposits, coordination as required by our account manager, and file all reports as required.

Budgets: Work with the manager to prepare annual budgets for all departments.

Cost Control and Cost Management: Work with the manager to consult and brainstorm on cost control, efficiencies, cost savings, and cost management. Prepare cost analysis on all aspects of the business.

Asset Management: Maintain lists of all assets and work with the manager to prepare and maintain asset management plan, execution, follow up, and updating.

Inventory and Supplies: Work with the manager and other departments to create inventory and supply plans and to ensure these are kept up to date, inventory is adequately supplied and well-managed, and supplies are readily available. Work with the manager to ensure all inventory and supplies are secured.

Workplace Safety: Be part of the ABC safety team. Liaise with safety agencies to ensure ABC is up to date on the latest requirements. Look after all reporting and remittance requirements.

Policies: Work with the owner, manager, and others to create policies for the business. Have all policies approved. Manage all policies and ensure employees are aware and informed of all policies related to their duties and responsibilities.

Taxes: Handle all postings, calculations, rebates, and remittances for taxes.

Communication and Reporting: Prepare all communication and reports for owners and manager as required. Issue reports and communication to staff as required. Respond to enquiries from staff, suppliers, etc., as required.

Accounting System: Enter all data and handle all bookkeeping aspects of the accounting system. Prepare monthly financial statements. Prepare annual financial statements for review by ABC's accountant. Prepare other reports requested by owner and/or manager.

Confidentiality: ABC is a private, family owned business. Confidentiality and discretion are an integral part of the business.

Other Terms and Conditions

Salary and Benefits: Hourly paid position at $XX.XX per hour to be reviewed annually. Benefits per ABC's standard benefit package after three months of continuous employment; employee contribution is required.

Hours of Work: This position requires flexibility but generally has a fixed work schedule. It is a full-time position of five days per week, eight hours per day, generally from 8:00 a.m. to 4:30 p.m. with a half-hour unpaid lunch break and two paid 15-minute coffee breaks.

Expenses: Expenses incurred will be reimbursed at cost and must be submitted to the manager for approval. We don't anticipate that this will happen very often.

Office Location: Your office is located in the ABC head office.

Annual Vacation: You will receive annual vacation in accordance with ABC company policy.

Statutory Holidays: Statutory holidays will be paid in accordance with prevailing laws and requirements.

Job Posting

Bookkeeper Position

ABC Company

ABC Company is seeking a bookkeeper for our small business. This position requires a person who is skilled and experienced in all aspects of bookkeeping, administration, policies, and office procedures. We are seeking an individual dedicated to his or her profession and desirous of a full-time career with a growing company in a growing industry. Applicant must have experience and possess a degree, diploma, and/or professional designation in order to be considered for this position.

Please reply by email to ABCcompany@email.com.

We thank all applicants in advance but only those selected for an interview will be contacted.

2. Be Thorough in the Interview

Applications will be received and prospects will be selected for an interview. You must prepare for the interview process then schedule selected applicants to interview for the position. When the applicants arrive for the interview you only have one chance to make a first impression. Remember, you are looking for the best applicant and he or she will no doubt have more than one job offer. You and your company will be on display for the prospective employee and you want the employee to have the best impressions of you and your company.

The interview process is critical. Your objective is to determine the best candidate for the position and for your business. You should be prepared with a list of questions and keep documented notes from all responses. If you have no employee interview experience, you may want to hire a professional or ask a knowledgeable person to help you.

Some companies have extensive interview policies and processes, which may include various aptitude and suitability tests. Your procedures need to be extensive enough to ensure that you are hiring the right person for the job. The person you hire may take over your company one day or work for you for decades. I have had both experiences numerous times and I am sure glad I took the time to hire the best people possible.

Small-business story

Our company needed to hire a new bookkeeper. We advertised extensively and had a list of ten qualified candidates, and we selected five candidates to interview. This was a critical position as the departure of our existing bookkeeper was imminent and we needed to fill the position in a timely manner.

Of the five candidates interviewed, one candidate stood out in the first interview. We invited that candidate in for a second interview. As the small-business owner, I was handling the interview and hiring process myself with a key employee in another department joining me in the interview. We were both convinced that we had selected the best candidate. I asked for references and they all checked out okay. We offered the position to this individual and we agreed on the terms, conditions, and start date.

We allowed for a training and transition period of one week. We believed this would be adequate due to the extensive experience of our new bookkeeper. Training week came and went and reports from the previous bookkeeper and the new bookkeeper were very positive.

On the second day that the new bookkeeper was working alone, he had a nervous breakdown. The job was too much for him. He walked out on us on the spot and left us in the lurch. We had to start the hiring process all over again and had to rely on our accountants to support us during this time.

What did I do wrong? I must have done something wrong, so I did some further research. I was misled not only by the prospective employee but by his references and finally the truth came out that this individual was not suitable for the position. If only I had taken the time to do a more thorough investigation when I had the chance. This mistake cost me time and money and put my company at risk for a month or two. I can tell you I have never made this mistake again.

Jack's response

Everyone who is involved in hiring has made a mistake when hiring a new employee; hopefully only once. But it does happen to us all on occasion. Be thorough throughout the entire hiring process and don't do management by wishful thinking. Just because you hope that this person will work out won't make it come true. If you want to hire the best employees, you have to have the best hiring practices. Don't be afraid to reject a potential employee if you have any doubts. Let your competitors hire your rejects.

3. The Relationship between the Employer and Employees

Now that you have hired a new employee, the relationship between you as the small-business entrepreneur and the new employee begins. You are the employer and the employee is the employee. You are not friends, you are not colleagues, and you are not equals. You have entered into an employer/employee relationship and if ever you allow the relationship to become anything but an employer/employee relationship, you are putting your company at risk and you are possibly relinquishing the control you must maintain over all of your employees. Remember that you retain the right to terminate the employment of any employee with or without cause. (**Note:** With cause and without cause dismissals should always be reviewed by legal counsel with experience in this area as the employee may be entitled to termination benefits under the law, even if the dismissal is for just cause.)

Assuming that you now have an established employer/employee relationship with your new employee, your next objective is to ensure the employee has the opportunity to be the best that he or she can be on the job. Regardless of whether an employee is the janitor or the assistant manager, your employee deserves the opportunity to perform to the best of his or her ability. Your obligation is to ensure that you provide the leadership, guidance, training, direction, communication, and objectives that will allow the employee to perform accordingly. Time invested in a good employee will pay huge dividends in the long run.

If ever you determine that an employee is not performing up to your expectations, you need to take action. Don't just sit back and complain about the employee; take decisive action. Meet with the employee, communicate, try to get to the bottom of the problem, restate your objectives and why they are not being met, explore options with the employee (maybe he or she is in the wrong job), and then give the employee the opportunity to improve and to help your company be successful. Be very clear about your objectives and the timeline you are allowing for improvement to be made. During this time, provide the employee with all the support you can. If after the timeline expires, and in spite of all of your efforts, the employee is still not making the grade, terminate him or her. You cannot build the A Team with B Team players. If you are happy to employ B Team employees, be prepared to be trounced by your competition.

As a small-business entrepreneur, a manager, and an employer, you have a huge responsibility when it comes to employees and you must respect, understand, and fulfil this responsibility. Employees are depending on you for their livelihood. Their families are depending on you to employ the breadwinner in their family. The employee's bank is depending on you to provide continued employment so your employee can pay his or her mortgage.

You should always be striving to be a good employer and the following are a few guidelines to achieve this objective:

- You are the employer and the employee is the employee — don't ever forget this.

- Never cross the line with an employee and blur your formal relationship; act professionally at all times.

- You are dependent on your employees and they are dependent on you.

- You have defined objectives that you want your employee to achieve; communicate your objectives and give your employee every opportunity to succeed.

- If you have a justifiable reason to terminate an employee, do so without delay. Don't make a mistake but don't delay either, your other employees will respect you for this.

- You are the boss, you are the employer, so give your employees all the reasons in the world why they should respect you by being a good leader.

- Give your employees the opportunity to communicate with their supervisors in a review process to ensure that both parties' objectives are being met.

- If an employee's career objectives and personal objectives (i.e., home life, income, family) are both being met and are in sync, you will have one happy satisfied employee who will perform to the best of his or her ability for the company.

- Things change in a growing company and sometimes employers cannot be everything to every employee. Sometimes employees have to change to make room for company progress and growth.

If you want to grow your business, you can't do it on your own. Every successful growing small business is dependent on their employees so if you want to be the best, start by hiring the best, then provide your employees with the opportunity to be their best.

If you want to be "employer of the year" in your industry or in your business group, please enhance your knowledge in employee relations far and beyond the space I have allocated for this subject. There are entire books written on employer/employee relationships.

Small-business story

My company was hiring for a reception position and we had selected the best candidate for a second interview. During the interview I discovered that the prospective employee was the sister of a very good friend of mine. My policy is not to hire friends or friends of friends but this person was by far the best candidate for the job. So for once, I decided to violate my own policy. It was one of the best decisions I have made in business. This person has held a key role in the company for the past 25 years and she will be celebrating her 30th anniversary with the company next year. Like I said, you can't build a successful company without great employees and this employee is one of the best, and has been instrumental in the company becoming the success it is today.

9

Account for It

First, you have to *sell it*; second, you have to *produce it for less than you sold it for*; and third, you have to *account for it*. This chapter will provide you with what you need to know about accounting for it and all the related paperwork.

1. Hire Someone to Help You

If you are a typical small-business entrepreneur and not trained as an accountant or a bookkeeper, the list of accounting requirements for your company should be enough to give you a headache. If you are trained as an accountant or a bookkeeper, you know and understand the meaning of all of these requirements. In order to be successful in business, you have to be adept at accounting and bookkeeping or you need to have a good working knowledge of all of the requirements. You may need to hire an accountant or a bookkeeper who is adept at accounting functions if you are not.

Let's assume that you are not a trained accountant or bookkeeper and you are going to hire someone to perform the accounting function in your company. This means that you still have to have a good working knowledge of all of these accounting requirements. How are you going to acquire this knowledge? The best advice is to take accounting courses, attend accounting training sessions, and read accounting-related books at the same time that you are learning the technical side of your industry. Remember you are not trying to become an accountant — that could take a number of years — you are acquiring enough knowledge in all aspects of the accounting function in your company so you know what your accountant, bookkeeper, and lawyer are talking about and so that you can give meaningful direction in this regard.

Typically a bookkeeper, either hired directly or under contract, can prepare monthly financial statements to meet your specific needs. The key is to know and understand how to read the financial statements so you can ask questions to better understand your financial position. Of course, it is extremely important for you to subject the financial statements to your own review to ensure that your bookkeeper is keeping and preparing accurate and reliable accounting information. Bookkeepers are not created equal so hopefully you have engaged a good one. If not, you could be headed towards Small-Business Hell.

In the beginning, ask your accountant to review your bookkeeper's work to ensure that you have engaged the best. Misleading financial information could result in you believing you are doing well when in fact you are losing money — a surefire way to go to Small-Business Hell.

Bookkeeping and accounting is done by computer program today and with your accountant's advice you can choose the program that is best suited to your business. Accounting programs, like bookkeepers, are not created equal and you need a program that is best suited to your business.

Small-business story

One of my key employees was stealing from me. It took me months to discover the problem but I finally caught this individual. How could someone I trusted and relied on steal from me? I had to fire him on the spot. I sought legal advice but the cost of pursuing this individual in court was not going to be worth the time or the effort. I can assure you he did not leave my employ with a good reference and I know this created some real hardship for him. However, I don't have any sympathy for him.

Jack's response

One of the most devastating things that can happen in business is when a key employee is caught stealing from the company. Every business needs to have policies and procedures in place to prevent theft but at the end of the day if someone wants to steal from you, the person will. One solution — always hire A Team players — they don't steal.

2. Invoicing and Collections

Invoicing and collections is an area in which a business can get into a lot of trouble if not managed properly. For example, poor billing practices will give your customers an excuse not to pay you on time. All of your financial commitments are dependent on billing your customers and collecting your receivables on time. This starts with good billing practices, invoicing to your customer's defined requirements, and insisting that you be paid on time in accordance with the terms and conditions you defined with your customer.

Note that customers may have specific coding functions or invoicing requirements that you must comply with and it's far better to get these defined up front rather than at the eleventh hour when you are waiting to be paid.

Before entering into contracts with any customers, and providing them with credit, you should have your potential customers complete credit applications. You will be filling out applications yourself when applying for credit with your suppliers so it is only fair that your customers complete them for your business. Granting of credit to customers is no different than you lending them money. You know a bank isn't going to lend you money without an application and provision of credit information so you shouldn't be expected to grant credit to your customers unless they are willing to undergo a credit review prior to you granting credit. You can avoid credit to your customers by insisting on prepayment, deposits, credit card on file, or payment on delivery.

There are exceptions to every rule and if you are dealing with someone you know or a very reputable company, you may want to forgo this procedure. If you are dealing on major capital projects, you will also want to investigate who is providing the financing and ensure that your customer's financing is secure.

If a customer doesn't pay in accordance with agreed-upon terms and conditions, what do you do? First of all, don't wait and assume everything is okay; communicate with your customer and get to the bottom of the problem. You have entered into a contract and you expect your customer to honor his or her commitment and this must be communicated clearly to your customer. If payment is not forthcoming, you will have to investigate builders' liens, legal action, or other methods of collection. Remember, for every dollar you don't collect from a bad, nonpaying customer, you will have to do even more work for good, paying customers just to break even.

The best remedy for this problem is due diligence prior to entering into a contract with your customer. If your customer is extremely belligerent or difficult when it comes to credit terms, maybe you should forget this customer and move on to customers you have more confidence in. Even good customers can get themselves into difficulty at times so be aware.

3. General Accounting

As mentioned earlier, you will want to use one of the common accounting programs that are available online or from stationery stores. These programs have different features and one may be better suited to your business than the other. Every bookkeeper today uses one or more of these programs and as you are doing your investigation into bookkeepers you can investigate the best accounting software for your business.

Do not agree to any form of custom software or nontraditional software programs. You will live to regret it but only after you've wasted thousands of dollars. Stick to the standard programs that are available and to bookkeepers who are familiar with these programs. Job costing for a contractor is a key feature of some programs so if you envision that you will be using the job-costing feature, make sure that your bookkeeper is familiar with these requirements.

If your plan is not to hire a bookkeeper, be prepared to go to night school to learn the program of your choice. All good accounting programs provide all aspects of general accounting including payroll, accounts receivable, accounts payable, checks, and payments. Most programs will provide additional software to allow your accounting program to do payroll and deal with federal, state or provincial, and local payroll taxes.

4. Banking

How much money do you need to operate your business? That certainly depends on what kind of business you have as well as the payment terms and conditions from your customers and suppliers, and other commitments and requirements. The key is you don't want to be overexposed to debt. Your accountant can advise you in this regard but a good rule of thumb is you should have one dollar in equity for every dollar in debt you take on.

How do you start your business when you have limited capital to invest? Start small and build your business on retained earnings. There are also the options of applying for a line of credit, capital bank loan, and mortgage:

- **Line of credit**: An agreement with your bank to allow you to overdraw your account by an agreed-on maximum amount. The line of credit debits and credits can be handled automatically by your bank to save you from having to manage it on a daily basis. Be aware that the agreed-on line of credit may be subject to margin requirements and other conditions as discussed below.

- **Capital bank loans**: Used for acquiring equipment and other large capital expenditures. These come with specific terms and conditions and the lender will usually secure them with security agreements and similar documents. You can talk to your banker or lender about these types of loans.

- **Mortgages**: Typically this is for real estate acquisitions. Commercial mortgages can have different terms and conditions than residential mortgages so make sure you are aware of all the terms and conditions before agreeing to a loan of this nature.

- **Margin and other loan commitment requirements**: Your bank or lender will want the loans secured in a number of ways. You can expect your bank or lender to provide you with a sheet outlining terms and conditions for your loan. In the case of a revolving line of credit, you may need to meet certain margin and other requirements in order to access your loan. For example, your lender may only allow you to draw your line of credit to a maximum of 75 percent of your current accounts receivable; therefore, you can only margin your accounts receivable to 75 percent.

Every business needs a bank and an account representative with some degree of knowledge about your business and banking requirements. If you are operating on your own financial strength, and you don't need a line of credit or overdraft protection, good for you! However, if you are like most businesses, you will need a line of credit from your bank to accommodate your business's financial commitments.

Your bank is in business to make money and the best way it can do that is to deal with good customers it knows are financially secure and will be able to repay the debt. Your bank is not prepared to take all the risks; it expects you to put money into your business and to possibly provide personal guarantees for any loans that it makes to your company. Your bank will always be more than happy to deal with you as long as you are making money and fulfilling your commitments to the bank. If you are in default, don't expect a lot of sympathy from your bank. Make money, retain your profits, and fulfil your commitments so everything will be good.

The bank will also expect you to provide accounting information on a regular basis; your bank will provide you with its requirements. Usually this includes monthly reports that would include in-house prepared financial statements, accounts receivable, payable listings, and work-in-progress reports. Annual reporting would include financial statements that may need to be prepared by your accountant.

Personal guarantees are your bank's way of attaining additional security and assuring that you are really committed to the success of your business. As soon as you sign a personal guarantee, you have put a lot more on the line than you may think. Stack up a bunch of personal guarantees from your bank, leasing company, and major suppliers and you are more than committed, you have put all of your personal assets at risk. This is the tipping point for many small-business entrepreneurs and the point at which you may be putting the well-being of your family at risk.

Your personal guarantee may also involve your spouse or partner and he or she may have to sign a guarantee as well. If this is the case, the bank may require him or her to seek independent legal advice (without you being in the room) so he or she is advised of the risks of signing a personal guarantee.

By agreeing to personal guarantees signed by you and your spouse is a huge commitment from not just you but your entire family. Personal guarantees can be reduced or eliminated if your borrowing requirements are small. Instead of growing your business with bank debt, grow your business with retained earnings. If you believe the risk of taking on a higher level of debt is to your benefit because you can take on more work, then be fully aware of the consequences if anything were to go wrong in your business.

Small-business story

I had an established line of credit for my business from a very large bank. We were going through a recession at the time and business was very tough and very competitive. I was doing OK though, having secured a contract that would carry us through for the next few months and hopefully to the point where the economy was going to improve. Out of the blue I received a call from my bank advising me that effective immediately my line of credit was going to be cut in half, and when the person said "immediately," the bank meant immediately. The reason? Head office no longer wanted to deal with small businesses in our geographic area in our industry. Payroll was the next day and the bank bounced my entire payroll. I spent the entire weekend borrowing money and securing funds so I could meet my payroll obligations. I was immediately thrown into Small-Business Hell and apparently there was nothing I could do about it. It took me months to recover from this debacle.

Jack's response

Obviously this business was overextended and had inadequate working capital. Retained earnings should have been left in the business, working capital targets should have been maintained, and the bank's margin and ratio requirements adhered to. In this case they obviously weren't, otherwise the bank would have provided the small business with time to make alternate arrangements. If you are relying heavily on bank debt, you are taking a huge risk in your business.

5. Costing

Are you making money on every transaction in your business? How do you know? Accurate and reliable accounting reports are important for you to successfully manage your business. They are also mandatory; the alternative is management by wishful thinking in which you think things are going along just great when in fact you are losing money. Cost reports can be prepared for every aspect of your business by coding sales and costs. Your bookkeeper can provide you with the reports you need that will allow you to analyze the various divisions or parts of your business. There is no use in making money on one side of your business and losing it on the other. For those of you in the construction industry, please read *Faster, Cheaper, Better*, which has much more detail on cost accounting and job costing.

6. Asset Management

From day one in your business you are going to accumulate assets. How you manage your assets is critical to the success of your business. Your accountant can advise on how you should manage your assets per various classes for tax purposes. What I am referring to here is how you manage your assets to benefit the day-to-day operation of your business. Obviously you should only be accumulating assets that will provide benefits to your business — in the short term and the long term.

You are the only one who can determine the benefits and make the best decision for your company. With all major equipment there are options, which can double the cost; therefore, all of this must be taken into consideration when making a buying decision. For example, you can walk into the showroom of a dealership and look at a very nice $20,000 truck that will meet your buying objectives but by the time you leave you have spent $40,000 with all the added extras the salesperson offers you. How can your business justify an additional $20,000 capital investment that will provide no benefit to the company?

The next decision is how you plan on paying for your purchase. Here are your options:

- **Cash:** Paying in cash uses up working capital. You'll need to consider whether or not the business can afford to have working capital tied up in major equipment assets.

- **Finance:** Typical options are through your bank or vendor financing which can be very competitive.

- **Lease:** Businesses today will lease you anything you want under a number of term options. If you are not careful, you can end up with an abundance of leases and the resultant long-term liability to which leases bind you. Have your bookkeeper carefully manage lease commitments by creating a lease-commitment report. This will keep you abreast of lease termination dates, optional or mandatory buyout terms, and other commitments under the leases. To lease or to buy is a decision best made after consulting with your accountant.

- **Rent:** Do you really need to own an asset or is renting a viable option?

When you have made a decision to acquire a piece of major equipment, you will need to consider maintenance and service. The cost of purchasing major equipment is only part of the story. You have to look at all costs throughout the life of the equipment.

Don't forget disposal costs because at the end of the useful life of the equipment you will have to dispose of it. Every small-business entrepreneur who has retired believes that all the equipment he or she has acquired over the years is worth hundreds of thousands of dollars, when in fact every potential purchaser is typically prepared to pay pennies on the dollar for used equipment. This is not always true when it comes to specialized equipment; however, it is almost always true when it comes to common equipment. Be prepared for this day so you won't be shocked. This bit of reality has to be taken into consideration when acquiring major equipment.

From an accounting point of view all capital assets are depreciated; meaning that their value goes down over time. Depreciation rates vary from asset class to asset class. Allowance for depreciation per asset class is a function that can be handled in your chosen accounting program.

7. Financial Reporting

Every accounting program on the market will provide you with a range of reports; in fact, too many to read or consider. In business you need clear and concise information that is accurate and reliable. You don't want to miss anything but summary reports are much easier to read and absorb than multipage reports that you may not want to take the time to read. You have to remember that financial reports are produced for your benefit and the information in the reports is designed to help you manage your business better and to keep you from going into Small-Business Hell.

You can't let the abundance of reports overwhelm you or unnecessarily tie you to your desk. Work with your bookkeeper and/or accountant to create reports that are clear and concise and that will provide you with the most benefit. Remember, if you spot an issue, or there is a concern, you can ask for additional information of which there will be lots available. The key reports you do need to be intimate with include the following:

- Monthly financial statements.
- Monthly financial summaries which can include an abundance of summary information:
  - Sales summaries.

- Work in progress.

- Marketing summaries.

- Accounts receivable.

- Accounts payable.

- Personnel (e.g., number of employees, new hires, and layoffs).

- Inventory.

- Job-cost reports prepared for each project.

- Summary job-cost report and work in progress.

- Aged accounts receivable lists.

- Aged accounts payable lists.

8. Cash Flow

Cash flow is a projection of how funds are going to flow through your company or bank account over a period of time, typically for a month, but could be for any specified period of time and projected forward for up to a year or more. For each month you are going to start the month off with some money in the bank. During the month you are going to have withdrawals for costs and expenses and deposits for payments from customers. At the end of the month you will have a new bank balance. What happens throughout the month with withdrawals and deposits defines your cash flow.

Sample 6 illustrates accounts receivable collected on time. Sample 7 shows a situation in which the receivables were not collected on time. Please note the extreme difference. Receivables must be collected on time in order for your business to function.

A cash-flow statement will provide you with other information as well as including the need for working capital, the need for an arranged line of credit at the bank, and when suppliers will be paid.

In the download kit you will find a Cash-Flow Statement that you can print or save on your computer to help you keep organized in your business.

Sample 6
Cash-Flow Statement with All Accounts Receivable Collected on Time

Description/Month	Jan	Feb	Mar	Apr	May	Jun	Jul	Aug	Sept	Oct	Nov	Dec
Opening Bank Balance	50,000	55,000	60,000	65,000	70,000	75,000	80,000	85,000	90,000	95,000	100,000	105,000
Withdrawals for Wages	30,000	30,000	30,000	30,000	30,000	30,000	30,000	30,000	30,000	30,000	30,000	30,000
Withdrawals for Other Project Costs	50,000	50,000	50,000	50,000	50,000	50,000	50,000	50,000	50,000	50,000	50,000	50,000
Withdrawals for Expenses	10,000	10,000	10,000	10,000	10,000	10,000	10,000	10,000	10,000	10,000	10,000	10,000
Withdrawals for Mortgages and Loans	5,000	5,000	5,000	5,000	5,000	5,000	5,000	5,000	5,000	5,000	5,000	5,000
Deposits from Customer Sales	100,000	100,000	100,000	100,000	100,000	100,000	100,000	100,000	100,000	100,000	100,000	100,000
Closing Bank Balance	55,000	60,000	65,000	70,000	75,000	80,000	85,000	90,000	95,000	100,000	105,000	110,000

The banker is happy because your account has a positive balance each and every month, because your receivables are collected on time each month.

Sample 7
Cash-Flow Statement with Some Accounts Receivable Not Collected on Time

Description/ Month	Jan	Feb	Mar	Apr	May	Jun	Jul	Aug	Sept	Oct	Nov	Dec
Opening Bank Balance	50,000	55,000	50,000	35,000	10,000	- 25,000	- 70,000	- 115,000	- 135,000	- 105,000	- 75,000	- 20,000
Withdrawals for Wages	30,000	30,000	30,000	30,000	30,000	30,000	30,000	30,000	30,000	30,000	30,000	30,000
Withdrawals for Other Project Costs	50,000	50,000	50,000	50,000	50,000	50,000	50,000	50,000	50,000	50,000	50,000	50,000
Withdrawals for Expenses	10,000	10,000	10,000	10,000	10,000	10,000	10,000	10,000	10,000	10,000	10,000	10,000
Withdrawals for Mortgages and Loans	5,000	5,000	5,000	5,000	5,000	5,000	5,000	5,000	5,000	5,000	5,000	5,000
Deposits from Customer Sales	100,000	90,000	80,000	70,000	60,000	50,000	50,000	75,000	125,000	125,000	150,000	100,000
Closing Bank Balance	55,000	50,000	35,000	10,000	- 25,000	- 70,000	- 115,000	- 135,000	- 105,000	- 75,000	- 20,000	- 15,000

The banker is unhappy because you have not collected your receivables on time and your account is overdrawn.

In this scenario, if the bank will not accommodate your overdraft, you won't be able to pay your suppliers and meet other commitments; your business will be in trouble.

Bottom line: You must collect your receivables on time.

10
Suppliers

Suppliers, wholesalers, jobbers, and distributors are just a few of the names used for material and equipment providers. Some of the names are unique to specific trades but for sake of clarity I will refer to them collectively as "suppliers," and everything provided through the suppliers as "material," even though the supply may go beyond material to include equipment, tools, consumables, and other project requirements.

Unless you are strictly a labor broker, suppliers will be an integral part of your business. As contractors and service providers, the reselling of materials is a major part of the business. Labor and materials make up the majority of costs on a project. For many businesses the cost of materials can exceed the cost of labor.

In the absence of material there is nothing you can do. You can have all of the other resources accounted for and in place but if you don't have the materials you need, where and when they are required, your productivity on the project will grind to a halt, which is a way to begin your journey into Small-Business Hell.

Your suppliers are in business to make money just like you are. You are their customer and, much like in your business, their objective is to meet your project objectives. For the most part, your supplier's role may be less complex than the role you play on the project in that the supplier is typically "supply only," but without your supplier meeting its commitments you won't be able to meet your customer's project objectives. Your supplier wants to meet the objectives you have defined. The supplier wants you to be a happy repeat customer and the best way it can accomplish that is to meet your objectives.

These are the typical objectives that you define for your suppliers:

- Meeting the scheduled delivery date.

- Competitive pricing.

- Quality materials and service.

What else could you ask for? You can summarize these supplier objectives as schedule, price, and quality. Do these objectives look vaguely familiar to Faster, Cheaper, Better? That's right. You want the same thing from your suppliers as you have committed to providing to your customers: Faster, Cheaper, Better. If your supplier's commitments to you are in line with your commitments to your customer, and your supplier meets all of its defined objectives, then that is a major step towards helping you meet your Faster, Cheaper, Better objectives.

If your customer's objectives aren't identified and documented, there is a chance that they won't be met. This applies to your suppliers as well. You and your supplier need to communicate so that the supplier can identify and document your objectives. Failing that, how can you expect your supplier to meet your objectives?

How well do you understand your supplier's business? Most suppliers are just that — suppliers. They are not manufacturers, although they may provide a range of supplementary services. Therefore, your supplier buys supplies, equipment, tools, and products from manufacturers or major distributors and resells these products to you. Most contractors are too small to deal directly with manufacturers and factories so the supplier's role is key as the middleperson between you, the contractor, and the multitude of manufacturers that build the materials and equipment that you need for your projects.

Imagine the number and quantity of materials it takes to put together one project. Even a small project may take hundreds of parts to complete. Major projects could have hundreds of thousands of parts if not millions. Every part has to be purchased, shipped, managed, and installed. It is absolutely amazing when you think of all the components of a major project. From the smallest nuts and bolts to major steel girders; from dozens of kinds of nails to a multitude of sizes and lengths of lumber; from drywall to plaster; from light switches to toilets; from pipe to concrete. The list is infinitely long. If you are missing one properly sized nut and bolt, a portion of the project could come to a halt.

This should give you a better idea of just how important your suppliers are and the importance of your relationship with your suppliers. Behind the counter at your suppliers' are representatives with knowledge about hundreds of thousands of parts and you need these representatives to help wade through the intense maze to get you exactly what you want, on schedule, and at a competitive price. Your suppliers and their representatives have no problem with this challenge. This is their business; this is what they do. They should be doing their business in the same professional manner as the way you are managing your business.

Looking at the industry from your suppliers' point of view, what do they want in their relationship with you? To do a lot of business with you would be the obvious answer. However, they want more than that, they want the same things in their business relationship with you as you want with your customers. They want business that they can establish and to have a good relationship with you as a customer; they want to meet the objectives you have laid down for them; they want to profit from their relationship with you; and they want to be paid in accordance with the terms and conditions of their sales agreements with you. If all of these things happen, you've created a win-win situation between you and your supplier. This will go a long way in helping you meet your project objectives for your customers.

The supply chain is not that long. It basically starts with manufacturers, then suppliers, then contractors, and then the end user. If there is any break in the chain, the end user is the ultimate loser.

Most suppliers' corporate structures are multibranch, located throughout their service areas. Their service areas could be local, state or provincial, and multi-state or multi-province. Most suppliers work on tight margins so the more buying power they have, the better prices they can offer to their customers. Quality service, quality products, and reliable delivery are the mantra of most suppliers; hence, Faster, Cheaper, Better. Because of their corporate structures, most suppliers are larger companies that may be independently owned or they may be part of multinational organizations or public companies.

Small-business story

I always dealt with one firm for the supply of my inventory. They always treated me well and met my objectives. One day, in my efforts to ensure I was getting the best price, I sought pricing from other suppliers. One supplier in particular offered me incredible pricing with the promise of the same quality and schedule, so I thought I would give it a try. This little experiment would prove to be very costly. The supplier's quality was poor, it never delivered on schedule, and it nickeled and dimed us to death for every extra cost you can imagine.

Jack's response

When assessing proposals from suppliers there is one thing we all know and that is one is less than two; in other words, we know who has the best price. Determining who has the overall best proposal requires a lot more than just looking at the price and the decision maker must have the ability to assess the overall proposal, not just the price, if all objectives are to be met without fail.

1. Supplier Credit

Many suppliers have policies in place that cover most aspects of their business. One of these policies is credit. Your supplier's credit policy will dictate the amount of credit your supplier is willing to grant you and the terms and conditions of that credit. Your supplier typically has limited ability to secure its credit position other than seeking personal guarantees and its ability to impose a builder's lien if it doesn't get paid.

Since your suppliers are one or two steps removed from the projects and end users, they aren't in an enviable position when it comes to the priority ranking of creditors. Your suppliers are well aware of their position in this regard and the risk they take in granting credit. Obviously your suppliers have a vested interest in the way you manage your business and in your success. If you are running a well-managed and profitable business, your suppliers are well assured that they are going to be paid on time. If you read, understand, and implement the business practices in this book, you are going to have a well-managed and profitable business. Therefore, your suppliers have a vested interest in you applying the business practices of Faster, Cheaper, Better.

Suppliers, collectively, write off millions of dollars in bad debts every year. Behind every bad debt is an unfortunate story where something has gone wrong.

Being a good customer for your suppliers means you are going to be the beneficiary of preferred pricing, preferred service, and quality supplies. However, if you have a deteriorated relationship with a supplier, all of these benefits go south and your business will be affected. This means from day one in your business, one of your primary business goals must be to maintain good relationships with your suppliers and this always starts with you paying your suppliers on time in accordance with their payment terms. If you miss payments, always pay late, and put your suppliers at risk of not getting paid, you will face the brunt of an organization that no longer wants to do business with you. Losing good suppliers is going to make your life very difficult when it comes to meeting your customer's project objectives.

Your suppliers are your partners in ensuring you can meet your project objectives. Similar to any good partnership, there must be respect, understanding, commitment, and communication, which are all very valuable components in a good and long-lasting relationship. Make it a priority to have a great relationship with your suppliers and you will derive the benefits, every day, in your business career.

11
Partnerships

Most small businesses have one small-business entrepreneur who owns the business. Some have two partners or more.

As soon as I start writing about partners in a business I have to explain my "complexity index." Essentially the complexity of any group of people is the square of the number of people involved. Therefore, a sole proprietorship with only one owner has a complexity index of one. Two partners in a business have a complexity index of four; three partners have a complexity index of nine; etc. You may think this is an exaggeration of what takes place in partnerships, but trust me the complexity index is a real indication of the issues businesses must face when there is more than one owner.

If there is only one owner in a small business, all decisions fall to that one person and everyone in the business and even customers know who ultimately makes all of the final business decisions. You can't get any simpler than that.

Introduce a partner into the business and this arrangement is four times more complex. I have had extensive experience in numerous business partnerships all the way from two partners to eight partners and I have also been a sole proprietor. It is this experience that led me to creating the complexity index and I have used this indicator to help guide many of my business decisions.

My complexity index also explains why governments have so much trouble getting anything done. Put ten politicians in one room with a complexity index of 100 and they will be hard pressed to get anything done or come to a common agreement on any subject.

The second part of the complexity index is that the complexity of the business structure should not exceed the complexity of the business itself. If you are going to start up a fairly basic small business, do you really want a partner or should you just go it alone?

That being said, there are still some reasons why a small business may want to have more than one owner or partner:

- Financing and/or business capitalization.

- Complexity of the business.

- Specialized skill set of each partner.

- Succession planning.

- Geographic considerations.

To have a partner or partners is a decision you must make. You just need to be aware of the complexity that you will be introducing into your business when you bring in a partner. Other things to consider that partnerships must deal with include the following:

- Partners will typically want to draw the same salary and this could put a burden on the business, especially a start-up business.

- In all partnerships there is the nagging question as to which partner is working harder, contributing more, making more money, spending too much, or taking more time off.

- Spouses will have their say even if they are not involved in the business, and inevitably they will believe their partner is contributing more than the other spouse's partner.

- Profits will be shared amongst partners so if you have one equal partner, you will be sharing the profits equally or profits may be shared proportionally by agreement or share ownership.

- Involving family members in your business when you have a partner is a very complex matter; children are not all created equal and this may be an issue.

Small-business story

My son was working in a related industry but I thought it would be a good idea for him to join my business. Unfortunately, he didn't have any postsecondary education; he just had his grade 12. Regardless of this disadvantage, I went ahead and hired him.

He did not report to me directly; he reported to one of my partners. After a few years I had plans for my son in the business but my partner fought me every inch of the way. In the end my son had to leave the business as this was the best decision for him. For me, I am still upset with the way things turned out. What did I do wrong? Maybe I shouldn't have brought my son into the business in the first place. My relationship with my partner over this matter is still a very sore point for me.

Ask yourself the following questions:

- Why do you want a partner?

- What will your partner bring to the business — special skills that you don't have?

- Could you consider hiring an employee to assist with the business rather than bringing in a partner?

- Will the partner you are considering make an equal contribution to the business?

- If your partner is bringing the same skill set to the business that you are, then why would you want to bring in a partner?

- Are you compatible with your proposed partner?

- Do you and your proposed partner have the same work ethic, business ethic, and belief?

- Does your proposed partner have any physical, mental, or substance abuse issues that could negatively affect the business?

- Are two heads better than one in the case of your business?

- Will a partner reduce or eliminate identified risks in the business venture?

Small-business story

My partner of ten years left his wife and took up with a new woman. His new girlfriend basically took over his life. Within one year he wanted out of the partnership, wanted to go on his own, and wanted to become my competitor. His new wife did not like me and I have to say the feeling was mutual. Our very successful partnership was over and I was forced to buy him out. The lesson that I learned is that people change and nothing is predictable in a partnership.

All partnerships need a partnership agreement that must deal with all partnership-related matters. Don't leave anything to your imagination, make sure your partnership is documented and agreed to. Legal advice is imperative when signing any contract. Partnership agreements should address all of the following:

- Share ownership or division of ownership.
- Compensation for partners.
- Distribution of profits and/or dividends.
- Buy/sell arrangements if one partner is leaving the business.
- Information on what to do if a partner becomes incapable of participating in the business.
- What happens when there is a death of a partner.
- Description of how to deal with irreconcilable differences.
- Funding of losses in the business.
- Succession planning.
- Minority shareholder rights.
- Clearly defined positions and responsibilities.
- Retirement instructions.
- Family involvement.

These are just some of the issues that should be dealt with in a partnership agreement. Again, legal advice is imperative.

There have been lots of successful business partnerships in both big and small businesses; there have been some significant failures as well. Take all of this into account before you make a decision as to how your business should be structured.

Small-business story

My friend and I decided to go into business together. He had no money so we borrowed money from my father. We had all of the loan documents and agreements drawn up by a lawyer so everything was legal and my father's investment was protected. The business didn't do badly but after two years we decided to wrap things up as it was a part-time venture for both of us and the business was becoming a burden.

On liquidating the business there was a shortfall in funding to pay back my father so my partner and I agreed on how we would make the repayments and who would be responsible for what. Although we had a legal document that supposedly covered all of these eventualities, I still had my partner sign a promissory note.

One year later my former partner refused to pay his share of the shortfall so I had to sue him. I consulted a different lawyer than the one we used originally. The first word of advice I received was that the original legal documents had been drawn up incorrectly and the only enforceable document was the promissory note that I had drawn up on the back of a sales contract. I was devastated, but luckily enough the hand-drawn document ruled the day and my former partner was forced to pay.

12
Competition

Competition is the foundation of our free-enterprise system. Take away competition and you have monopolies dominating the economy. Monopolies by their structure take away all of the incentives that drive the free-enterprise system. Can you imagine a business sector where one business dominates the entire sector and you have no choice but to patronize that business? What reasons would that business have to improve its service or meet your buying objectives? The answer is none.

Introduce competition and now what happens? You suddenly have choice. You can choose the business that is going to do the best job of meeting your buying objectives. If you don't like one business for whatever reason, you can go to its competitor.

As a small-business entrepreneur you should operate your business under the assumption that there will always be competition and your competitors would like nothing more than to take away some of your market share. They don't want to take away all of your market share or destroy your business; they just want to be the dominant supplier in the industry. Therefore, every day in your small business you should be doing the same thing. You should always be striving to be better than your competition.

I have a funny saying that I use quite often when I am talking about my competition: "Happiness is my competition in my rearview mirror!" What I mean by this is I want my competition behind me trying to catch up. While my competition is trying to catch up to me I am forging ahead and doing everything I can do to keep my competition behind me.

Good competitors are good for business and good competitors will stay in business. Bad competitors will come and go, will upset the marketplace, and will ultimately go out of business. No matter what happens in business, there always seems to be one or two bad competitors competing for your customers' business.

Small-business story

When I finally retire the one group that I am sure to thank will be my competition. Of course I will thank my partners, our employees, our suppliers, our bank, and others but I will reserve some real praise for my competitors. At the end of the day it was my competition that really forced me to be the best that I could be and to be the best choice for my customers.

Your job is to earn your customers' business and we certainly covered that in Chapter 4: Meeting Your Customers' Objectives. Just as there are bad competitors there are bad customers and sometimes they deserve each other. If a customer wants to choose your competitor over you when you know full well that your proposal or product is superior in every way, then there are times when you can't do anything about that. You can only hope that your customer, having had experience with your competition, will return to do business with you at the first opportunity. When this happens it will prove to you that your commitment to meeting your customers' buying objectives every time will pay huge dividends over time.

You will likely get to know your competitors through trade associations, industry groups, trade shows, and community events. Always remember that these are your competitors. They are not your friends. They are not your colleagues. They are not someone you should confide in about your business. They are your competition. You should always treat your competition with respect but never forget that they are your competitors and their job is to take away your customers.

I believe competitors and competition are responsible for the success of every small business. As a true small-business entrepreneur you are a competitor, and you want to win. You know you won't win every time but you want to be the most successful small business in your sector. You are constantly striving to be the best that you can be, such as being the most innovative, having the best ideas and service, employing the best employees, and being the firm that is managed better than any of your competition.

Note: Be aware that price fixing and collaboration with a competitor is against the law. The free-enterprise system is dependent on the free-market system that must be protected from collusion, price fixing, and noncompetition agreements. Never stoop to the level of cooperating with your competition. Always do your best to compete in the marketplace at all times.

One rule that I follow is that I never mention my competitors' names in the presence of my customers. My competitors have no right to be discussed when I am meeting with my customers. If I am not going to mention my competition by name, that means I am not going to comment on them — good or bad. They are totally out of my mind when I am meeting with my customers. If customers ever ask me about my competition, I will never say anything derogatory, I will only say that they are good competition or they are competitors. I want to win the business for my company by demonstrating to my customers how good my business is, not how bad my competition is. Good customers will respect you for this and will support your business accordingly.

If you stay in business for a period of time, you will inevitably find that you will be competing with former employees. Employees from time to time quit and set up their own businesses or they go to work for your competition. What do you expect? After all, you trained them very well. When a former employee becomes a competitor, he or she will use what he or she learned in your business to compete with you. The advantage that you have is that your business is always moving forward and becoming more innovative so if your former employee is trying to steal your business ideas, they may be old ideas by then.

Small-business story

One of my employees quit out of the blue. This person was a good employee that may have had a future in our company. He quit to go work for one of our competitors who wanted to expand his business in our field. This employee obviously took ideas from my company and immediately started to use marketing materials that were exact copies of materials that I personally had created. I said to myself,

"How low can a person stoop in business?" Obviously this former employee had very low business standards.

We stood our ground with our customers and although this new competitor did take away some of our business, it was out of business within one year and moved out of our area all together. This was very positive in the end because this former employee who quit is not someone I would want involved in my business. So much for him, but who is going to be next to try me on?

13
Risks

Everything we do in life involves risk. All risks cannot be eliminated. Some risks can be avoided while others cannot be avoided but they can be managed.

Most of us go through our day-to-day lives not thinking too much about risk. Most of us eliminate many risks in life by not pursuing a career as a tightrope walker or race-car driver. Most of us avoid risks that cannot be eliminated; for example, we can't eliminate the risk of walking down the street but we can avoid the risk of getting run over, by properly crossing at the marked crosswalk. Risks that cannot be avoided can be managed such as wearing your seatbelt when you drive your vehicle.

Risks in business are like risks in life. Everything we do in business involves risks. All risks in business cannot be eliminated; however, some risks in business can be avoided while others cannot be eliminated or avoided but they can be managed.

The difference between everyday life risks and business risks is that we have a lifetime of experience on how to identify risks in life; but if you are new in business, you don't have any experience on how to identify business risks. A business risk that isn't identified cannot be eliminated, avoided, or managed; it will be waiting there to poke up its ugly head and bite you in the butt when you least expect it! A risk that is identified can possibly be eliminated, avoided, or managed.

1. Identify the Risks

Your job is to identify risks in your business and then determine how to deal with the identified risks. This is important to remember: Risks in business that are not identified cannot be eliminated, avoided, or managed.

This is what you need to consider when you have identified the risk:

- Can the risk be eliminated? If so, develop a plan to eliminate it.

- Can the risk be avoided? If so, develop a plan to avoid it.

- Can the risk be managed? If so, develop a plan to manage it.

The following sections identify the most common risks to business in the selling, production, and accounting phases. This is not an exhaustive list. The objective of this chapter is to teach you how to identify the most important risks so you can eliminate, avoid, or manage them. These are the consequences of not eliminating, avoiding, or managing risk:

- Not meeting your customer's buying objectives.

- Financial losses.

- Financial disaster.

- Small-Business Hell.

2. Selling It Risks

The following sections will help you identify the "selling it" risks. They give you guidance on whether or not to eliminate, avoid, or manage the risks.

2.1 Misunderstanding customers' buying objectives

Eliminate this risk: Do a thorough job of understanding and documenting your customers' buying objectives. You will find very quickly and with experience that you will be able to lead the understanding and documentation process with your customer and I can assure you that this will put you into a preferred position with your customer.

2.2 Customer misunderstandings about objectives and pricing

Eliminate this risk: Do a good job of documenting your customers' buying objectives and follow up with clear and concise pricing information.

2.3 Underestimating the cost of what you are selling

Manage this risk: This risk cannot be eliminated or avoided in its entirety without making your pricing totally uncompetitive. Use accurate and reliable historical cost records and your business experience to ensure that you prepare an accurate and reliable cost.

Small-business story

My customer called and said my price was too high on a project that we had worked on getting for over a year. The customer had decided he was going to go with the low price unless I could convince him otherwise. He asked me to meet him but when I learned the extent of the discount he was looking for I walked away. This decision still hurts many years later but it was a decision I just had to make. My company's well-being and profitability had to come first.

2.4 Bidding too low

Avoid this pitfall: Assuming you have prepared an accurate and reliable cost estimate, the risk of bidding too low for a project remains in your hands as to what is a fair markup for the sale. You want to be competitive but you have to make a fair and reasonable profit. If your competitors want to do the project for no profit, let them.

2.5 Lack of understanding of complexity and unforeseen conditions

Eliminate this risk: You have to take the time and use your experience to ensure you understand the complexity of what you are bidding on and have the vision to foresee conditions. If you can't eliminate or avoid the risk, manage it by identifying the risk in your project objectives and put in conditions that ensure that you will not be damaged or hurt if the risk occurs. For example, if the sale has a very tight schedule and weather is a risk, put into your conditions that the schedule will be adjusted for production days lost or affected due to weather.

Dependence on other suppliers is almost always an issue so when others fail to meet their schedule objectives, be sure to include a condition that will adjust the schedule for situations like this.

2.6 Lack of resources to undertake your commitments

Manage this risk: On any given sale you are committing to provide all of the resources to the customer, which they have purchased. At this stage you need to know that the required resources will be available when needed. Labor shortages and material delivery delays can all have an extremely adverse effect. Unfortunately this risk cannot be totally eliminated or avoided so you have to manage it.

During the selling phase, investigate the availability of required resources such as labor, materials, subcontractors, and other costs. Potential resource shortages identified at this stage can be managed and/or accommodated within the cost estimate and/or conditions.

2.7 Issues with subcontractors and suppliers

Eliminate this risk: The best way to avoid this risk is to only use subcontractors and suppliers that you know will meet all of their objectives. Surround yourself with good suppliers and subcontractors. One bad subcontractor or supplier could put the entire sale off the rails. This risk must be eliminated. If you are contemplating using subcontractors or suppliers who you are not familiar with, research them before you commit to using them.

2.8 Unscrupulous customers

Eliminate this risk: Believe it or not there are unscrupulous customers out there. You don't want to do deal with these types of customers. Check out your potential customers and make sure they are upstanding, creditworthy, and people with whom you want to do business. If you have any doubts, say thanks and pass on the opportunity.

2.9 Poor relationship with the customer

Eliminate this risk: You must believe that you can develop a good relationship with your customer. If you don't believe you can develop a good relationship, you should pass on doing business with this customer. You need to focus on customers who you believe will appreciate the unique and extraordinary approach that you will bring to the sale.

Customers who can't see beyond the lowest price are going to have a tough time appreciating your commitment. Price is extremely important, but there is a lot more to a sale than a low price. Your best customers will recognize this; these are the customers you need to focus on, and eliminate all the rest.

2.10 Lack of vision

Eliminate this risk: You need to have a vision for the sale you are pursuing. You need to envision schedule risks, cost risks, and quality risks. You never want to say to yourself: "I never thought of that." You need to eliminate this risk to the best of your ability by using your experience to envision potential risks and then take appropriate action.

3. Cost Risks

The following sections will help you identify cost risks. They give you guidance on whether or not to eliminate, avoid, or manage the risks.

3.1 Not meeting your customers' buying objectives

Manage this risk: This is one of the biggest potential risks of all. The customer could have 100 buying objectives and if you fail to meet just one of them, the sale could be a disaster. Meeting your customer's buying objectives doesn't mean meeting *some* of the objectives, it means meeting *all* of your customer's buying objectives. For example, a baker preparing the biggest and nicest wedding cake of his career in which he met all of the bride's objectives except for the schedule; he delivered the cake the Monday after the wedding. The fact that he met 99 out of 100 objectives wasn't good enough. The customer needed all of her objectives met.

Manage this risk during the selling stage so that all of the objectives are identified and documented.

3.2 Sale mismanagement

Eliminate this risk: It is management not mismanagement that is the key to success. Sales can be mismanaged for any number of reasons but the reasons are only excuses. When it comes to sales management don't accept excuses only accept results. Eliminate this risk by making best management practices in your business mandatory and accept nothing less under any circumstances.

3.3 Not providing Faster, Cheaper, Better service

Eliminate this risk: You are committing to an overall Faster, Cheaper, Better service and sale when compared to your competitors. Eliminate the risk of not meeting the objectives of Faster, Cheaper, Better by adopting this policy throughout your company. Ensure all your employees are trained in these practices and, above all, manage your business using these three objectives.

> **Small-business story**
>
> *We had just bid a major project and had gone through an extensive interview and review process. The customer then called and told me I was the preferred bidder but my price was too high and could I offer a small discount. This was a competitively bid project so my first inclination was to say no but we really needed this job. We had done a very good job demonstrating to the customer that we were going to be Faster, Cheaper, Better but he wanted us to be a little bit Cheaper. I finally agreed after a lot of soul searching. This turned out to be a very good decision. But if the customer had pressed me too hard I would have had to walk away no matter how painful it would be to lose the sale.*

3.4 Not producing the product or service for less than you sold it for

Eliminate this risk: Not making a reasonable profit should be a criminal offense. You are in business to make money, not to lose money. Everything you do from the minute you start work in the morning to the time you quit for the day has to focus on making a reasonable profit on each and every sale.

3.5 Inaccurate and unreliable cost-to-complete estimates

Eliminate this risk: This is one of the greatest risks in business. An inaccurate and unreliable cost-to-complete estimate on a sale could send the entire sale off the rails. You may believe you are on track to making your estimated profit but in fact you are destined to lose a substantial amount of money, which means you are totally misguided. Only an accurate and reliable cost-to-complete estimate can provide you with the information you need in order to effectively manage the sale to ensure the sale meets all of its objectives. Eliminate this risk by ensuring the sales manager has the skills, abilities, vision, knowledge, and facts in order to prepare accurate and reliable cost estimates. This is one of the most important management tools you can have.

4. Account for It Risks

The following sections will help you identify the "account for it" risks. They give you guidance on whether or not to eliminate, avoid, or manage the risks.

4.1 Undercapitalization

Eliminate this risk: If you are undercapitalized and have overextended yourself, even though you may be making a profit on your sales, you could be putting your company at risk. If you have all of your capital tied up in accounts receivable and no funds available to make payroll, you are going to be in a lot of trouble.

Eliminate this risk by seeking professional advice to determine capitalization requirements for your business and then maintain the required capital in your business. Don't take on sales that have the potential of overutilizing your available capital.

4.2 Not getting paid by your customer on schedule

Eliminate this risk: You can be doing everything else right but if your customer doesn't pay you on time, you are not going to be able to fulfill your commitments. Your bank is not going to lend you any money against overdue receivables.

This risk must be eliminated by ensuring invoices are issued accurately and in a timely fashion in accordance with the project terms and conditions and you must insist that your customer pay you on schedule. If, for any reason beyond your control, your customer doesn't or can't pay you on schedule, you must be prepared to take appropriate and immediate action.

4.3 The customer has financial difficulties

Eliminate this risk: This is a call you never want to get: "We are sorry but we just went broke and you are not going to get paid." Believe me, this happens.

This risk must be eliminated at the selling-it phase to ensure that you are offering your services only to customers who are financially stable. For every dollar you don't collect on an account receivable you have to do about $20 in business just to get back to even. Not a good prospect. You are fulfilling your obligations and you deserve to get paid; that is the deal and any other alternative is not acceptable.

4.4 Personnel problems

Manage this risk: Human resource (HR) matters can be infinite in number; for example, alcohol and drug issues, family problems, poor performance, lack of initiative, poor training, unsafe work practices, insubordination, and lack of respect. This list can go on and on.

Manage this risk by hiring first-class people. There is an old saying that first-class people hire first-class people and second-class people hire third-class people. Go first class! Employ great HR practices, and ensure you are hiring the best people for the job. In today's economy you are likely going to pay a poor employee about the same as a good employee so you may as well hire the best from the get-go.

4.5 Inaccurate and unreliable cost reporting

Eliminate this risk: Applying an accurate and reliable cost estimate to inaccurate and unreliable cost reports will result in disastrous misinformation. Accounting and bookkeeping must produce accurate and reliable information that responsible personnel and the project manager can rely on and trust. Consistent misinformation from the bookkeeper will skew the entire organization and head the business towards Small-Business Hell. Eliminate this risk by employing the best skills in bookkeeping and accounting and demand accurate and reliable information.

14
Family

Many small businesses are family businesses. It is amazing how many children follow in their parents' footsteps in business. Sometimes this can be a good thing and sometimes not. Note that the complexity index I introduced in Chapter 11 certainly applies to family businesses as well.

It is only natural that family members are attracted to the parents' business. My father was an electrical contractor and this is the career goal that I followed. I took my apprenticeship with my dad but I quickly learned that once my training was complete I did not want to stay in his business. This arrangement was not going to work for me. For many small businesses, family is a key part of it and ultimately the succession plan.

Small-business story

Dad: My son asked me one day, "Dad, what do I need to do to have your job?"

I said, "My job requires a professional designation so first you have to get your degree in business, then complete your internship, and then get your professional designation. After you have done all that, when I retire you can apply for my job but it will be up to the other partners to decide whether or not to hire you."

Son: I followed my Dad's advice and got my professional designation and all the experience I needed in order to take over my Dad's job. My Dad's retirement date was coming up and the firm advertised for my Dad's position and I applied. My Dad made it clear that I would be on my own and he wouldn't influence the decision to hire me. I guess I impressed the other partners because I was offered the job and took up my new position upon my Dad's retirement. Today I am a partner in the firm and this was the best career move I could have made.

In many small businesses the children of the owner grow up with the business. There is always an opportunity for children to train in the business, to learn about the business, and to help out where needed. It just seems to be a natural progression. But whether to involve your family in your business is a very big question for every small-business entrepreneur.

Small-business story

My dad tried to encourage me to join the family business. He had a good business but it wasn't for me. I was honest with my dad and the family and everyone agreed with my decision. Instead I went to university and became a teacher and now I am retired after a 35-year career in the field of education. However, it worked for my brother; he joined the family business and had a successful 35-year career as a small-business entrepreneur.

If you believe that you want to involve family in your business, here are some things that you should ponder:

- Is this the right decision for your son or daughter or other family member? The decision for the family member to join the business should be his or hers and the person must believe it is the best thing for him or her and his or her career.

- Don't let a family member into the business unless he or she is prepared to qualify and/or obtain the education needed in order to participate equally in the business with other employees.

- Don't give a family member a job just because you feel sorry for the person. You will live to regret that decision.

- Are you prepared to fire a family member if the person doesn't perform or meet your expectations? No one should be exempt from being fired if he or she doesn't perform well.

- If ever you have to fire a family member, are you prepared for the consequences? Many a family has been torn apart because of family business disputes.

- Can you work with a family member in the business? It is extremely difficult to balance work and family. Will you be talking business at family events when you should be focusing on the event and not the business?

- If you are going to involve your spouse in the business, how is this going to impact your relationship? Can you separate business from your personal lives?

- Who is going to look after the business if you are a family business and you all want to go on a family vacation together?

- Will the business take over and dominate your family and everything the family does?

- If you involve more than one family member, will there be sibling rivalry? As family members progress, who will report to whom? Will this be a manageable situation?

- Consider having a family member leave the business for a period of time to gain experience from related businesses or even other industries.

- Will your employees discriminate against your family members? It does happen.

Small-business story

My husband started his own business and since I was a trained accountant it only made sense that I get involved in the business with him. Two years later the business was destroying our marriage and our personal relationship so I quit. That's right. I quit working for my husband and it was the smartest thing I ever did. We are still married and my husband still has his business. We may talk about his business from time to time but his business no longer dominates our life. Thank goodness for that!

15
Succession Planning

You have spent years building a successful and profitable small business. Now what? What are your plans for succession and retirement? This is a question that you must ask once you realize that you have a small business that actually is a success and a business that has future value for someone. This chapter discusses the common concepts of succession planning.

1. Family

Family members joining the family business was discussed in Chapter 14, but here is some additional information. If you have made the decision to involve family in your business, you will need to consider whether or not they are going to be part of your succession plan. This is typically not a decision that can be made in the early years. No family members should be expected to take over and run the family business unless they have the training, skills, qualifications, education, wherewithal, experience, and personality traits required in order to be successful and be able to run the business profitably.

It is amazing how many family members follow in the footsteps of the family business. You have likely seen a number of businesses named "Jones and Son," or "Smith and Daughter," or other similar family named businesses. It is obviously a natural progression for many small businesses to become family businesses whether by plan or by happenstance. No family members, though, should be forced into the family business; it should be by choice and it should be the best choice for the family members coming to work for the business.

The concept of families can transcend small business as many large businesses have family members involved as well. For example, the Ford Motor Company has had Fords at the helm for almost its entire history. We all know Donald Trump has involved his children in his business empire. If it's good enough for the Fords and the Trumps it should be good enough for small business as well.

Small-business story

Father: My son worked for me for four years and became a fully qualified tradesperson while in my employ. During this time he was taking all kinds of business courses and industry-related courses. He was definitely grooming himself to take over the business. Unfortunately, I never discussed any succession plans with him.

One day my son came into my office and gave me three months' notice that he was leaving and moving to another city with his wife and my grandson. I don't think my son had any idea that I had plans for him and, once he made up his mind, there was no changing course.

Son: Working for my father wasn't going to work for me. He had a vision that I would work and he would play golf. That was not going to happen. My dad did provide me with a very solid foundation to be successful in my field.

If you are going to involve family in your business, what are your expectations? What are the family members' expectations? Do they expect that you will hand the business over to them one day on a silver platter? Or is this just a job and they have no expectations to run the business or take it over one day? There are a lot of questions that need to be asked but they can't necessarily be asked on day one when the family members join the company. It may take years for them to prove themselves and gain the experience they need in order to take over the business.

This is why we call it succession planning; "planning" being the key word. A succession plan should be discussed and considered five to ten years before the time you are actually thinking about retiring or changing career paths.

As part of your five-year business plan you will need to introduce the concept of succession and if you believe family members could be part of the plan, you will need to have this discussion with them. This is a real case of planning for success, not for failure. Projecting five years may seem like a long time but it is very important to open the conversation now to ensure that any contemplated plan will work for both parties. Your expectation and your family members' expectations may be many miles apart and you will never know this unless you have the conversation.

Small-business story

I was grooming my son to join my professional practice. I thought it would be great to pass on my business to my son one day when I retire. Since I am a professional, it required my son to obtain his professional degree. Once he obtained his first degree, he called me up one day and said he wanted to follow a different career path in construction — a career that is totally opposite from my professional career! What could I say except that I would support his decision all the way?

Today my son has his own very successful small business in the construction field. He wears blue jeans and a safety vest every day, whereas the life I envisioned for him would have meant a suit and tie. My son is extremely happy. His business is doing very well. I think over time he is going to make more money as a construction contractor than I did in my career as a professional.

My succession plans changed overnight. It worked out okay as I was in a partnership and ultimately my partners were able to take over my business and clients. As the saying goes, "All is well that ends well."

If the business is a professional business and a family member wants to join, obviously the person is going to have to obtain his or her professional designation and the onus is strictly on him or her to achieve this accomplishment. If you are a small business that does not require a professional designation, does this mean you should let a family member join the business without a business diploma, business degree, or other relevant education? Why should a business have lower standards for admittance to it just because it is not a business that requires a professional designation? My recommendation is that you require any family member who wants to join the business to have a business or industry-related diploma or degree. Why not? Every community in

North America has access to colleges and universities that offer business and industry-related training. Don't ever allow a family member to join the business unless he or she first proves himself or herself in the field of education and training. Lowering the bar for family members will undermine your business and will not inspire your other employees.

If everything works out and family members work for your small business, and you believe one or more of them has the interest and is capable of running the business, you could introduce them into your five-year plan after you have explored the options with them and given them the opportunity to express an interest in pursuing the idea of taking over the business.

Your expectations must be very high and at some point in time your expectations must be written down and agreed to by all parties. If the transition is five or more years away, you have a lot of time to work towards the defined objectives.

As the plan proceeds, you will need legal and accounting advice and prospective family member partners should seek independent advice from professionals. You absolutely want your family members to be walking into any arrangement with you with their eyes wide open, leaving no chance for misunderstanding. All agreements must be in writing; leave nothing to chance.

Now that you have considered a succession plan with family, you must consider other options as well. There are many things that could happen and change in your life as well as your family member's life that could put any transition plan in jeopardy. For example, what if the family member being groomed to take over your business wins the lottery? Not a very likely scenario but one more thing that needs to be considered. What if someone was to die or become incapacitated? This unfortunate circumstance must also be taken into consideration. Planning ahead can make sure the business is in safe hands if the unexpected happens. You must have a backup plan.

Small-business story

My dad was grooming me to take over his business and everything was going along quite well; we had a plan. My dad had a few more years to go before retirement so I had lots of time to learn from him and learn how to run the business. Then my dad had a heart attack and died at the age of 55. I was devastated, my family was devastated, and I was thrown into running the business, on my own,

*overnight. I am happy to report that I survived, the business has done
well, and I thank my dad every day for the few short years he took me
under his wing and trained me.*

2. Partnerships

Partnerships are a very popular and successful way of succession planning, if done the right way. If you started your business with a partner and you are both about the same age, your succession plan will likely have you both retiring and leaving the business at the same time. If one partner is older than the other, the succession plan may involve the younger partner succeeding the older partner in the business. Maybe the succession plan is to introduce more partners into the business allowing the older partners to retire while the business carries on being run by the younger partners. There are myriad possibilities for succession planning within a partnership.

Again the most important aspect of succession planning is the plan itself. At some point in time almost everyone wants to retire or wants to change the course of his or her career. Succession planning with a partnership can offer a number of advantages if they are planned.

If your business is structured as a partnership, you may want to make an expanded partnership part of your succession plan. I like the idea of the "decade plan." This is a plan where you develop future partners, when the possibility exists, who are 10 years younger than the older partners, and 20 years younger than the older partners. This is obviously not a pure science as you don't want to promote someone into the business just because of their age, but everything being equal, why not give the younger generation the opportunity? When it comes time for the older partner to retire there will be young fresh blood ready to take over. If you are able to implement the decade plan, you are setting your business up for longevity which is one of the key components of a successful, long-term business plan.

Buy-sell agreements, which are an essential component of every partnership agreement, have a succession component within the plan as the agreement contemplates various scenarios of what happens when a partner wants to leave or retire from the business. A better plan is to contemplate succession within your five-year business plan to allow you to explore all opportunities for succession, not just the trigger clauses contained within a buy-sell agreement.

Small-business story

My business partner and I had a great business. We were good at it, we both worked hard, and we profited for the benefit of ourselves and our families. Life was good. My partner's wife worked for the business, mine did not. We had come to this arrangement by mutual agreement and it worked very well for both of us; she was very good at her job and my wife had other interests.

One night we got a phone call. My partner and his wife were in a car accident and she was killed. I will never forget that phone call. I was immediately thrust into Small-Business Hell. And then things got worse. My partner never really returned to work. He started drinking heavily and had to leave the business, forcing me to buy him out. These were very tough times. I can tell you our five-year business plan did not contemplate this disaster. Nevertheless, I survived and was able to get the business back on a sound footing within a year, but it took a lot of hard work and dedication on my part; the journey was rewarding in the end. My ex-partner died far too young with a broken heart and a damaged liver. Life can be tough some days.

3. Sale of the Business

Your succession plan can be accomplished by simply selling your business. Sometimes this can be achieved quite quickly with great results but more often than not the sale of a small business can be a real challenge. If your business is in demand and it is salable, this may be the most opportune way to achieve your succession objectives. However, this is not always the case. For example, there was an old plumber who thought his inventory, tools, and vehicles were worth a fortune. When it came time to sell, he was in for a painful surprise.

Small-business story

My grandfather started the business in the 1930s, then my father took over, and then 30 years ago my brother and I took over the business. The business has steadily grown over the years and expanded into the development and sale of high-tech manufacturing equipment. The business has always been focused on one segment of the industry and over the decades we have had our ups and downs with the ever fluctuating price of this industry's commodity. We were able to survive with hard work, dedication to the business, and smart business practices. A few years ago we were approached by a large public company and it bought us out for millions. Now my brother

*and I are retired and we thank our grandfather for starting the busi-
ness. Sometimes family businesses do work out.*

There are so many things to consider when selling a business:

- Is the purchaser buying shares in your business or assets only?
  Clarify this before you do anything else.

- What is the purchase price and how is the purchase price to be
  allocated? You will need professional tax advice in this regard.

- Is the buyer going to pay you for goodwill; in other words, your
  legacy of having a good reputation with your customers?

- If you consider vendor financing, have you evaluated all the
  risks? Do you have all of the documents and security in place?
  Under the terms of most vendor financing, you may end up with
  the business back if the buyer defaults.

- Do you have contracts in place with key employees or can they
  leave the new buyer once the sale has closed? The employees
  may have allegiance to you but not to the new owner.

- Are there contingent liabilities for you and the buyer to consider?

- If you are offering any guarantees, have you fully analyzed the
  risks associated with this kind of arrangement? What would happen if you are offering a guarantee related to a customer and then
  the customer reneges on an order? Does this put you at risk?

- If your business name is your family name and the new owner
  fails in business, is this going to adversely affect your reputation? You may insist on a name change, albeit minor.

The bottom line is you should seek accounting and legal advice
from professionals with expertise in this field. Remember that not all
accountants and lawyers are created equal. Some are better than others, so seek the best advice.

Small-business story

*I finally sold my business after months of trying. I was ready to retire.
I was a little bit desperate so I agreed to take on vendor financing with
a small downpayment. Everything went well for the first six months,
then the buyer decided he didn't like the business so he just walked
away and left me in the lurch. I went back in and ran the business for a
few months but I just didn't have the same enthusiasm and the buyer*

who left me high and dry had lost some of my best customers due to bad service. I had no choice but to shut down the business and sell all my assets at bargain-basement prices.

I went from Small-Business Heaven to Small-Business Hell overnight and now my retirement is not what I had imagined. I should have started my succession plan five years ago not one year ago. If I had done this, I am sure things would have turned out differently for me.

4. Employee Buyout

Employee buyout is a very popular way of succession planning. At least you know who you are selling to and you know the person has the experience to operate your business. Like everything else in business, employee buyouts come with risks and challenges and these must be identified and managed within the agreements. Many of the same questions that were contemplated in a sale to a third party need to be considered in an employee buyout. Remember, you are not selling to friends or colleagues; you are selling to a third-party buyer who just happens to be your employee or employees.

Most importantly, you want a sale to an employee to be a success for him or her and for you. You should never consider an employee buyout unless you are convinced that the business will succeed under this new ownership. Remember that once the sale is complete, the employee will instantly become a small-business entrepreneur. This could be a good thing, but will the person be able to handle this monumental change in his or her life and assume risks that an employee would never have to consider?

Another consideration is that an employee buyout group may contain employees you know are not the right choice. The group as a whole may not realize this. You may have to play a leadership role and guide the buyout group as best as you can. Remember, you want them to succeed and no one knows better than you what it takes to be successful. Give them every chance to succeed as well.

5. Business Wrap Up

The final alternative is for you to wrap up your business. You may want to do this for any number of reasons. Most importantly is that a business wrap up does not need to involve a third party. You are in control of the process and you make it happen. Again, be aware that many of the assets that you may have considered valuable may be worth very little when they go under the auctioneer's gavel.

Even though this is a very simple method of planning your retirement, there may be contingent liabilities when you wrap up your business. Check with your legal and financial professionals to make sure you do everything right. You don't want to be relaxing on a beach somewhere after retirement and get a call from the tax auditors telling you that you didn't file all the right forms.

6. Valuing Your Small Business

The true value of anything can only be determined when a buyer and a seller agree on a price that has been determined in a competitive marketplace. What do you think your business is worth? What would a buyer think your business is worth? The answers to these questions are dependent on a multitude of criteria:

- What is the buyer buying? This must be defined.

- What is the potential earning capacity of the business?

- What is the goodwill value? Goodwill is the most nebulous part of any small-business sale discussion.

- What are the prospects that customers will continue to do business with the new buyer?

- Will all the key employees stay with the business or is there any risk that they could quit the business and go into competition with the new buyer?

- If employees are to be terminated and lose their jobs when the new buyer takes over, who is responsible for any severance pay or salary and benefit continuation?

- Have all contingent liabilities on the part of the seller and the buyer been considered, identified, and agreed to?

- Who is responsible for taxes, of all kinds, on completion of the sale?

- Who is responsible for legal fees, selling fees, and accounting fees for the transaction?

- Is the sale subject to any subsequent events? If so, these must be identified, discussed, and agreed to up front.

- How are inventory and other similar assets to be valued at closing?

- The transition of licenses, approvals by authorities, and operating certificates must be addressed in any sale agreement.

- If vendor financing is under consideration, the seller and buyer must be totally aware of all the risks associated with this type of arrangement.

- If there are items that are not to be part of the sale, these must be identified and agreed to.

- Work in progress must be valued and the method for valuation must be agreed to.

- Prepaid expense valuation must be valued and agreed to.

- If this is an internal sale to new partners or family members, the seller must be prepared to disclose all pertinent information — nothing can be held back.

- Who retains the working capital, retained earnings, and bank accounts?

- If the business has debt, who will be responsible for this debt?

- If the seller has provided personal guarantees or other types of guarantees, the release of these guarantees must be dealt with and all releases confirmed in writing.

- If you are considering special selling arrangements for family members or employees, in the case of employee buyouts, make sure these are fully understood by all parties.

- The seller and the buyer may wish to consider independent third-party valuations of the business.

As you can see, there are many items to consider. Only professionals with experience in the sale and purchase of businesses should be consulted to ensure that all documents and agreements are correct and legal. A word of warning: Professionals are expensive and representatives of the seller and the buyer can spend an inordinate amount of time trying to come to an agreement on your behalf. The seller and the buyer know what they want to accomplish and this needs to be clearly communicated to all advisors; otherwise, professional costs could easily get of hand.

For many of us small-business entrepreneurs, the ultimate sale of our businesses can be a significant part of our retirement plans. Make sure you consider this when putting together your succession plan. Remember the word "plan" is key to achieving your objectives for your ultimate departure from your business.

16
Small-Business Hell for the *New* Small-Business Entrepreneur

I hope you have enjoyed reading this book. As you will know by now, I am not trying to scare readers and aspiring small-business entrepreneurs. This book is all about providing entrepreneurs with guidance to be the best that they can be in their chosen professions. In the case of new small-business entrepreneurs, I want to make sure you have the tools to succeed from day one in your business.

I have no interest in scaring aspiring small-business entrepreneurs out of going into business. Where would commerce be without small businesses taking the risks to go into business for themselves? A world without small business would be a world dominated by conglomerates and that would be a world where none of us would want to live.

That was my pep talk for going into business; this is my pep talk about how to stay in business. Like I said earlier in the book, setting up a small business is easy — almost anyone can do it. The tough part is to stay in business and make money.

New small-business entrepreneurs are especially vulnerable when it comes to risks that could send them into Small-Business Hell. The words of advice in this book, if followed, could help you eliminate some risks and could help you identify and manage risks that cannot be eliminated. I am sure that almost all new small businesses will make some mistakes. Some of these mistakes may be serious enough to put the business into Small-Business Hell.

You are going to make mistakes. It is these mistakes that are the foundation of your experience. Let's assume that in your first year of business you do 50 major things right but you make 50 mistakes along the way. That's okay. Just make sure that you learn from every one of your mistakes and that you don't repeat them. If you make the same mistake twice, you should reread this book.

In your second year in business, keep repeating the 50 things you did right in your first year, and based on your newly discovered experience, try 50 more things. Of those, 25 may work well and 25 may be mistakes. Going into your third year in business, you can rely on 75 proven things you have done right and only have to try 25 new things of which probably only half will work again. You get the idea. After five years in business you should know what to do, what not to do, and you should be making money and have a great business.

What happens during your first five years in business if one or more of your mistakes is serious enough to send you into Small-Business Hell? This is a problem and likely the main reason why about half of new small businesses do not survive, for whatever reason, beyond their first five years in business. I want you to be a survivor and not be one of the unfortunate small-business statistics.

As you know, a problem has to be fairly serious in order to send you to Small-Business Hell but if it happens, what are you going to do about it?

The first thing to ask yourself is: Why did this happen? Is this a risk that you didn't foresee? Is this a risk that you couldn't eliminate? What is the risk associated with — sales, production, operations, or personal?

Depending on the cause of the catastrophe in your business, is there a solution? Even if it's a miracle that could happen, is there a solution? Now is the time to prepare a plan to move forward and get out of Small-Business Hell. The first thing you should do is review your five-year business plan. Your business plan did not contemplate going into Small-Business Hell so something has obviously gone amiss between development and execution of your plan in the real world of small business.

Is there a solution? Can you come up with a solution on your own? Do you need to seek professional advice to come up with a solution? If you do come up with a solution, and it works, how long is it going to take to get out of Small-Business Hell? Do you have the stamina, the commitment, and the willingness required to execute a solution and work your way out of Small-Business Hell? It is always a lot easier to get into Small-Business Hell than it is to get out of it.

If, no matter what you do you can't see any way that you can work your way out of Small-Business Hell, you will have to explore the exit criteria because you can't stay in Small-Business Hell forever. This never-ending trip into Small-Business Hell is all consuming and will destroy even the toughest small-business entrepreneur. Therefore, if you determine that there is no possible way you can work your way out, immediately seek professional help to guide you out of your business and back into a life of normalcy. If this happens to you, don't feel bad. Every successful small-business person hits bottom at least once and maybe this experience will help guide you when you next consider a venture into small business.

If you have come up with a plan to get yourself out of Small-Business Hell, good for you! Be prepared for some hard work and commitment to make the trip out successful. These may be the most trying times of your business career. If you are successful, this experience will be a positive in your overall business experience. In fact, this may be your one and only trip into Small-Business Hell. If this is the case, you learned enough in the first trip to ensure that you are not going back again no matter what!

Only those who have been to Small-Business Hell can really tell you what the trip is like. Devastating when you arrive, pure hell while you are there, and a huge sigh of relief and sense of accomplishment when you work your way out of it. Just make sure that you revisit your business plan one more time when you are out of Small-Business Hell and make the appropriate changes based on your very valuable experience.

If your plan to get out of Small-Business Hell is based on borrowing your way out, then make sure you think twice. Any funds you borrow will have to be paid back based on your business being successful. If you make this decision, with willing lenders, make sure you are proceeding with your eyes wide open and a fully revised business plan that takes this new debt into account.

Small-business story

My colleague and I decided to quit our jobs and go into business for ourselves. We had different trade qualifications that would complement each other. We were both very experienced and the market for our construction-related services looked promising.

It took awhile but we finally secured one large contract that would see us through for one year. That would give us a lot of time to look for more work and meet our sales objectives within our business plan. This was going to be a great project.

We were only 10 percent complete when we got a call from the general contractor and he advised us that the owner, due to slumping commodity prices, was putting the project on hold indefinitely and we should send in our bill for work completed to date. We were devastated. This was a disaster for our business. We were immediately thrust into Small-Business Hell. This is not a risk that we ever considered in our business plan. Even if we did identify this risk, I am not sure how we would have come up with a management plan for such a risk.

Unfortunately we were out of business within the month. We had just enough funds to pay off our debts and get out from under the business but we both still lost a lot of money. They say timing is everything and our timing, in this case, was lousy.

Jack's response

A very unfortunate story that has happened time and time again to small businesses that become totally or very dependent on one customer for all of their business. Your business plan should always contemplate a broader client base with limited exposure to one customer. This risk wasn't identified; therefore, it wasn't contemplated and managed. Unfortunately it cost these partners their business and personal investments.

17

Small-Business Hell for the *Experienced* Small-Business Entrepreneur

I consider the experienced small-business entrepreneur to be one who has been in business for five years or more. After all, five years is a long time in business and to have survived that long, a business must have done a lot of things right and been profitable along the way.

So why would an experienced small-business entrepreneur make a mistake or take a risk that could potentially put him or her into Small-Business Hell? The answer is usually based on the desire and need to grow and expand the business into new business opportunities.

Remember the story about Target's Canadian business venture? Why did Target even bother to go into the Canadian market? Certainly not to lose money and pull off one of the biggest business failures in Canadian business history! No, Target ventured into the Canadian market to make money and grow its business. Ask Target executives now how well this venture went.

The business plan, therefore, for experienced small businesses, should not be a shot in the dark or wishful thinking. A business plan should be based on sound business statistics, experience, and proven data. Almost every business plan projects business growth. Just like the government projects a growing economy, not a contracting economy, businesses like to project growth and improved profitability. It will take the following in order to grow the business sales and profits:

- New markets.

- New products.

- Expanded territory.

- Increased market share at the expense of the competition.

- Higher production efficiencies.

- Lower production costs.

- Acquisitions.

Big business has a history of debacles that has cost millions if not billions of dollars. Target is not alone in this department. In fact, there are so many on the Internet that I can't even comment on the number. Do a search and you will see what I mean.

While I was writing this book, the Volkswagen diesel engine fiasco was unfolding. In 2015, Volkswagen was accused of rigging diesel engine emission testing. It is unbelievable that one of the most profitable and successful automobile manufacturers in the world could be teetering on the edge of failure.

When will all these huge, devastating mistakes by big business ever stop? The answer is never! As long as the free-enterprise system and its investors demand ever-increasing sales and profits, businesses will be forced to take risks that may or may not be successful. Success could springboard the companies forward to new innovations, more growth, higher profits, and happy shareholders. Failure could devastate the companies, or at least have a significant impact. In the case of Volkswagen, we may never know what would drive such a well-respected company to seek success through devious, unscrupulous, and unlawful business practices. This will be a topic written about for years to come.

In the case of experienced business owners, we take risks as well in our pursuit for business growth in sales and profits. The key is to what extent you are prepared to go. What risks are you prepared to take in order to achieve this objective?

I have a saying in business and that is: "Do what you know, do it well, and do lots of it." There is comfort in this statement and following it does mitigate a certain amount of risk. However, if a business really wants to grow and expand its horizons, sticking to "what you know" is not always the answer. Sometimes you have to expand beyond what you know and this, in itself, presents a risk to the business. What degree of risk is the question? If the plan for business expansion and growth involves a risk of any magnitude, then the risks must be identified and analyzed. The best thing to do is a series of "what ifs":

- What if this new business venture was to fail? What impact would it have on the company as a whole?

- Could the company withstand a failure of this new venture?

- If the business venture were to succeed, will the benefits outweigh the potential risks?

- Does the new business venture put the business at risk in any other areas beyond financial (e.g., legal, ethical, and/or company mission statement being violated)?

- Will this new business venture put existing operations at risk?

- What impact will it have on existing infrastructure, operations, employees, and equipment?

- Are your bank and/or lenders supportive of the new venture?

- Is there a capital cost to setting up this venture? If so, how much and can the company afford to pursue it?

- Would your business need additional working capital? If so, what will the source be for it?

- Is the new business complementary to your existing business operations, or is it unrelated? The answer to this question is the key to addressing the related risk to this venture. For example, take a look at Microsoft's venture into the cell phone business and see how that went — a business that was unrelated to its core business.

- What impact will the business have on management resources? There is only so much time in the day, and only so much capability at the top.

- Who is in control of the new business venture? You, as the experienced small-business entrepreneur in an established business? Or are you a minority partner in the new venture?

- If you are acquiring an existing business in order to accommodate sales and profit growth, have you totally explored the acquisition, risks, benefits, and all the other related issues?

- Who is going to manage the new enterprise? Are they capable? Can they pass the small-business entrepreneur test?

There are an infinite number of questions that could be asked but the depth of the risk and benefit analysis needs to be equal to the impact it may have on the business. The most important thing is to integrate the idea of business expansion into the five-year business plan and then, and only then, make the decision as to whether this is a good decision for your small business. Remember, as an experienced successful small-business entrepreneur, you have much more to lose than you did when you were first starting out. You may have built up substantial assets and retained earnings, but do you want to put these at risk?

Now what happens if after all of this an experienced business ends up in Small-Business Hell? It does happen and I have to admit it has happened to me even with my decades of experience. For an experienced business there is typically only one answer: You must manage your way out of Small-Business Hell whether it takes a day, a week, a month, or a year. If you have followed all of my advice in this book and you still end up in Small-Business Hell, something devastating has happened that you did not contemplate in your business plan. It's time now for superior management skills to take over to get your business out of Small-Business Hell and back into the good business position you were in before you went down that road.

There is another business saying that says management should be spending 80 percent of their time on the 20 percent of the business that is causing problems for the organization. There is no better time to apply this management principle than now when your business is suddenly thrust into Small-Business Hell.

As an experienced small-business entrepreneur you may have opportunities, even when things are going bad, to change course and avoid the trip into Small-Business Hell. Sometimes this takes drastic action on behalf of management, but the decisions made at this juncture may be easier than the decisions that need to be made once you are actually in Small-Business Hell.

I have focused my reasons for a trip into Small-Business Hell on the need for business growth and increased profitability. Of course, there are many other things that could happen that would have a devastating impact on a business:

- Customer problems, which can be unforeseen.

- Supplier problems, which also can be unforeseen.

- Employee-related matters.

- New competition devastating the market.

- Changing times that should have be foreseen but weren't.

- Health issues for the small-business entrepreneur or partner(s).

- Death.

- Divorce.

- Addiction issues (e.g., alcohol, drugs, gambling).

- Family matters.

The list goes on and on. The bottom line is that the business plan needs to at least contemplate these things and determine a management plan for these issues.

18
Making Money

If you think profit is a bad word, then you have just wasted a whole bunch of time reading this book. Profit is not a bad word; profit is the lifeblood of every for-profit business. A business is in business to make a profit — not to lose money, not to break even, but to make a profit.

How much profit should you make? Personally I subscribe to making a fair and reasonable profit on each and every business transaction. In my opinion, greed is not a good business trait to have. Meager profit says, "Why are you bothering to be in business?" A fair and reasonable profit will ensure the success of your business and, more importantly, will be the driving force behind your commitment to make your business a success.

In order to figure out what a fair and reasonable profit is, research other businesses in your field and find out how much money they are making. Does five or ten cents on every dollar of business seem to be the average? For example, if you do a $100,000 in business, you should expect a minimum profit of $5,000 and potentially up to $10,000. If you do a $1 million of business annually, you should expect a minimum profit of $50,000 but a $100,000 profit would be much better. These levels of profit are not greedy; they are fair and reasonable profit expectations.

The profit I am referring to here is net profit before taxes but after all costs of sales and expenses are accounted for — including payment of wages or an allowance to the owners. Artificially boosting up profits by not paying yourself a reasonable wage is a false economy. There are things you may want to do for accounting and tax purposes, but at the end of the day, your net profit before taxes must be after you have allowed for a reasonable wage for the owner. For example, as the sole owner of your business, your sales are $1 million per year so you pay yourself a salary of $75,000 per year. You should earn a profit of between $50,000 and $100,000 for the year before an allowance for taxes. Now that is incentive!

How can you justify earning this kind of money? With your salary and your profit for the year described above you have effectively earned between $125,000 and $175,000. Does this sound unreasonable to you? All of your salary is your salary. If you weren't doing the job in your company, you would have to hire someone at $75,000 to do the job. Your profit is what you have earned in your business, a profit that represents a return on investment and a return on the business enterprise. By not paying yourself a fair wage, you are living in a false economy. If your company does not earn a fair and reasonable profit for the year, you are putting the company in jeopardy and into a position in which the company will not be able to prosper and grow.

As stated previously, profit is the life blood of any for-profit enterprise. Without profit, or with only a meager profit, an enterprise cannot grow and prosper.

1. What Happens to the Profits in Your Company?

In the early stages of your business, you likely want to retain the profits to build retained earnings, reduce debt, and increase working capital. Here is one more reason why you want to pay yourself a reasonable salary. You and your family can live off of your salary and the profit can be applied to the full benefit of the business.

Of course, a reasonable annual dividend or bonus paid to yourself for your extraordinary efforts throughout the year would certainly seem reasonable. When your family benefits from the profits in your business, they will better appreciate the "beyond the call of duty" efforts that you put into your business and they will realize they are worthwhile after all.

Ideally business growth should be fuelled by retained earnings and not the accumulation of more debt. Let's say that your business is doing $1 million a year in business and your business has $100,000 of invested working capital and a $100,000 line of credit. You would like to grow your business to $2 million a year in business so you should increase your working capital to $200,000 and you do this by building up working capital, by retaining your after-tax earnings in your company. You will find this method a lot easier than trying to borrow the $100,000 to grow your business. Growth by retained earnings is the best way to grow your business.

What happens over a period of time when you are no longer growing your business and your business has more than adequate working capital? What do you do with your profits? You should seek the advice of a professional accountant or an investment advisor. You have reached the pinnacle of success and you are now building some very serious net worth.

Am I telling you that your business, if successful, has the ability to make you wealthy? Yes, I am. You may have never had the vision of being wealthy and here you are, after a number of years of running your own business, you find yourself in a position of wealth. Amazing? No! Deserved? Yes!

The 80/20 rule can be applied to so many things in life and in business. I hold to the theory that 80 percent of the profits made in business are earned by 20 percent of the companies. This may be a stretch but it indicates that 80 percent of the companies are underperforming and not making the profit that they should. However, 20 percent of companies that are earning 80 percent of the profits are the stability of the industry, the most viable, the best run, and the most successful. Which group would you like to be in? If your company fits the profile, your company is in the elite 20 percent of companies that consistently earn profits in excess of 5 percent of sales each and every year. A very enviable position to be in! To those companies in the 80 percent group, it's definitely time to reread this book as well as *Faster, Cheaper, Better* and put into action the many good business practices that are advocated throughout. Work yourself up to reasonable profit expectations and join the elite 20 percent group.

Conclusion

For every Small-Business Hell story with a sad ending, there are many, many more that have a positive ending. This is a book about Small-Business Hell and how to avoid the trip, so many of my stories are based on bad business experiences. Fortunately, there are many stories and Small-Business Hell experiences with a happy and rewarding ending. No matter what happens in business, most small-business entrepreneurs come out of Small-Business Hell better for the experience. Unfortunately, this is not always the case and Small-Business Hell has devastated many. That's life in small business. Most small-business entrepreneurs can survive Small-Business Hell and benefit from the trip.

Having said all that, I still encourage you to avoid the trip to Small-Business Hell, if you possibly can, and I hope this book helps you achieve this objective!

Small-business story

I started my small business when I was quite young and just married. Two children later and with the success of my small business I was doing very well personally and in business. Life was so good I could see that I could retire early; ten years earlier than I had planned and there was an opportunity for me to sell my business. The next thing I knew the business was sold, I was retired with a five-year noncompetition clause, and life was still good.

One year later I was bored stiff. I retired way too early. What could I do? I guess luck was with me because the group that bought my business decided to break up the business and agreed to sell me back part of it and amend my noncompetition clause. I was back in business.

Fifteen years later and I am still not retired and our business keeps expanding. My children are involved in the business now, we have a great succession plan in place, and we continue to be very profitable. What else could a person ask for in the life of a small-business entrepreneur?

Download Kit

Please enter the URL you see in the box below into your computer web browser to access and download the kit.

www.self-counsel.com/updates/bus_hell/15kit.htm

The download kit includes:

- Entrepreneur worksheets

- Editable financial spreadsheets, purchase order, and job-cost estimate for use in your business.